WRITING ABOUT IMAGINATIVE LITERATURE

WRITING ABOUT IMAGINATIVE LITERATURE

Edward J. Gordon
Yale University

HARCOURT BRACE JOVANOVICH, INC.
New York · Chicago · San Francisco · Atlanta

ISBN: 0-15-597850-0

Library of Congress Catalog Card Number: 73-75180

Printed in the United States of America

PREFACE

This book has been planned to teach students how to write about literature. Although it contains a number of complete short stories, poems, and plays, it should generally be used along with a literature anthology or other more extensive readings. Its step by step presentation makes it especially valuable for the beginning student.

If the student is to write intelligently about any literary selection, he must first know how to read that selection with understanding. As he reads, he must ask the kinds of questions that a good literary critic asks. Each of the three parts of *Writing About Imaginative Literature*—The Short Story, Poetry, Drama—begins with an analysis of a selection. The selection is reprinted in full, and discussion and demonstration provide questions to be asked, answers to those questions, and ways ideas about the selection can be developed into essays.

Next, the terms used in discussing the particular genre are defined: such techniques as point of view, setting, plot, characterization, symbol, metaphor, rhythm, and theme are explained in simple language with examples from the selections in the text or with further short quotations. The student is then taken, step by step, through the problems of writing a paper: finding an appropriate topic, discarding inappropriate topics, developing the topic into a thesis, making notes on specific details that will support his statements, and classifying the notes in logical order. All these steps are illustrated with excerpts from selections included in the book.

Further, the student is shown how to begin an essay—with a note on openings to be avoided, how to choose an appropriate title, how to end a paper, and suggestions on proofreading the first draft. An appendix demonstrates how to introduce quotations into the critical essay.

After the student has been shown how to write a paper, a number of exercises give practice in writing different kinds of critical papers. The instructor will, of course, choose the exercises most suited to his particular course.

I wish to thank those who gave so much help in the making of this book: the staff of Harcourt Brace Jovanovich, especially William A. Pullin, Vice President, who proposed the idea, and Dorothy E. Mott and Susan Wladawsky, whose careful editing improved the manuscript; and Professors Laurence Perrine of Southern Methodist University, Gerald Levin of the University of Akron, and Selwyn Kittredge of Fairleigh Dickinson University, who read the early drafts with such helpful care and made so many constructive suggestions.

E. J. G.

CONTENTS

WRITING ABOUT IMAGINATIVE LITERATURE

INTRODUCTION

This book has been planned to help you write intelligently about short stories, poetry, and drama. It is based on the assumption that to write effectively about your reading, you must first understand what the author is saying; only then can you write in depth about what you have read.

Another assumption is that intelligent reading grows from the kinds of questions that you ask yourself as you read. A good critic is continually asking himself questions; he carries on an internal dialogue with himself as he reads. The quality of your questions, then, will control the quality of your reading.

Each section of the book moves from problems of reading to problems of writing. First, each genre (short story, poetry, and drama) is defined; then the major concepts that make up the structure are explained in some detail. Each division ends with a series of questions that will help you to determine how a piece of literature is put together. What the questions mean should be clear from the discussion that precedes each set. As you ask these questions, you are learning not only to read a particular work, but also to become a better reader of any work.

Next, you read a few selections and are asked to write about them. Though this book does not presume to be a handbook on writing, you are shown how to think about your answers and how to organize what you will put on paper.

The principles discussed here are common to most pieces of literature; yet since writers tend to experiment, you will find some exceptions. If you know what is customary, though, you will better understand the exceptions.

When we write about our experiences in reading, we are learning to put them in intellectual terms; we clarify our ability to think. Thinking entails seeing relationships between things and ideas and stating what those relationships are. Most of our thinking is done in words. We are never clear about what we think until we can express our thoughts verbally. The most exact expression of thought is in writing, if it is good writing.

Anyone who reads good books and writes his reactions to them will develop a respect for what words can do. Since much of what we learn is perceived through words, the meanings that we give to words help determine how we live. If a person does not look for the meanings behind words, for the reality that they stand for, he may acquire the inflexible belief that each word has one meaning. He will then be at the mercy of those propagandists who control others by eliciting stock responses to persuasive language. If a person *does* realize that a word has many meanings that can be worked out through the context in which it appears, he will be a controller of words, instead of being controlled by them.

The ability to control words comes when we realize how a good writer makes his complex organization of words, with multiple meanings and relationships. We will then realize that it is impossible to change a word or the position of a word in a sentence without changing the meaning of the sentence, even if only slightly. As we work out the complexities of a literary piece, we are also being brought into a wider world not available to those who do not read well. Reading good literature can help us to find true freedom.

All our lives we will be carrying on arguments about, for example, political, legal, or moral matters. When we write about our reactions to literature, we are learning how to argue. We are learning to state clearly what the argument is about, to clarify the meanings of our key terms, and to offer evidence for what we believe.

So reading and writing about literature are not merely concerned with some vague appreciation of beauty; we are called on to use our minds as fully as possible: to state a thesis to be argued, to define terms, to classify ideas, to generalize about specifics, to understand the nature of evidence. Thus, they help us to learn something of ourselves and others, of why people behave as they do. The skills of reading and writing are closely akin to the skills of competent living.

1

THE SHORT STORY

READING THE SHORT STORY

A short story is a fictional narrative in prose, ordinarily containing less than 20,000 words; anything longer might be called a novella. The story usually attempts to show what the leading character is like by demonstrating how he acts under some form of stress.

The author of a short story is not merely telling what happened; he is concerned with the meaning of the events as they relate to the character or characters, and he is interpreting the action. He chooses the events to show how someone acts under stress, selecting those crucial moments when a character must decide to act one way or another. The author deals with a certain portion of a person's life, but leaves out much more than he includes. If he were to tell everything that a person says, thinks, or does during a given day, the result would be longer than a novel and might have no significance. He selects what he thinks are the major portions of his story: the actions, the speeches, the thoughts of a person facing an important crisis. Selection, then, is one of the major techniques of the story writer. No word should be wasted; everything should be part of the main effect.

The story is usually built on a conflict to which the main character must react; when his reaction is ended and the results are obvious, the tale is told. How the character reacts to that moment of stress reveals a great deal about him. If his problem is one that many people face, the story takes on universality; it may also show us much about ourselves.

In reading a short story, we must talk to ourselves, asking questions that will help us to understand how the parts of the story are related to the whole, what the details add up to. The most important question is always "Why?" Why are we given this particular information at this time? Why has the author withheld other information?

The kinds of questions we ask are based on the critical vocabulary used in talking about fiction. As a football game is put together from such actions as blocking, passing, ball-carrying, forward passing, and the like, so a story is put together from devices that have been used by storytellers for more than two thousand years. If we understand how the techniques work, we are better able to understand the structure of the story. Then we are learning not just what one story "says," but rather how to read all short stories.

A writer is creating a world and asking you to enter imaginatively into it. You hear a voice (point of view) saying that something is happening (plot) to someone (character) in some time and place (setting), and that the action of the story illustrates a meaning or dominating idea (theme). Although it is difficult (often impossible) to separate the major elements from one another, we must try so that you may understand them.

To see how these basic parts of a story work, read the following selection and discussion.

THE PIECE OF STRING — Guy de Maupassant

It was market-day, and over all the roads round Goderville the peasants and their wives were coming towards the town. The men walked easily, lurching the whole body forward at every step. Their long legs were twisted and deformed by the slow, painful labors of the country:—by bending over to plough, which is what also makes their left shoulders too high and their figures crooked; and by reaping corn, which obliges them for steadiness' sake to spread their knees too wide. Their starched blue blouses, shining as though varnished, ornamented at collar and cuffs with little patterns of white stitch-work, and blown up big around their bony bodies, seemed exactly like balloons about to soar, but putting forth a head, two arms, and two feet.

Some of these fellows dragged a cow or a calf at the

end of a rope. And just behind the animal, beating it over the back with a leaf-covered branch to hasten its pace, went their wives, carrying large baskets from which came forth the heads of chickens or the heads of ducks. These women walked with steps far shorter and quicker than the men; their figures, withered and upright, were adorned with scanty little shawls pinned over their flat bosoms; and they enveloped their heads each in a white cloth, close fastened round the hair and surmounted by a cap.

Now a char-à-banc passed by, drawn by a jerky-paced nag. It shook up strangely the two men on the seat. And the woman at the bottom of the cart held fast to its sides to lessen the hard joltings.

In the market-place at Goderville was a great crowd, a mingled multitude of men and beasts. The horns of cattle, the high and long-napped hats of wealthy peasants, the head-dresses of the women, came to the surface of that sea. And voices clamorous, sharp, shrill, made a continuous and savage din. Above it a huge burst of laughter from the sturdy lungs of a merry yokel would sometimes sound, and sometimes a long bellow from a cow tied fast to the wall of a house.

It all smelled of the stable, of milk, of hay, and of perspiration, giving off that half-human, half-animal odor which is peculiar to the men of the fields.

Maître Hauchecorne, of Bréauté, had just arrived at Goderville, and was taking his way towards the square, when he perceived on the ground a little piece of string. Maître Hauchecorne, economical, like all true Normans, reflected that everything was worth picking up which could be of any use; and he stooped down—but painfully, because he suffered from rheumatism. He took the bit of thin cord from the ground, and was carefully preparing to roll it up when he saw Maître Malandain, the harness-maker, on his door-step, looking at him. They had once had a quarrel about a halter, and they had remained angry, bearing malice on both sides. Maître Hauchecorne was overcome with a sort of shame at being seen by his enemy looking in the dirt so for a bit of string. He quickly hid his find beneath his blouse; then in the pocket of his breeches; then pretended to be still looking for something on the ground which he did not discover; and at last went off towards the market-place, with his head bent forward, and a body almost doubled in two by rheumatic pains.

He lost himself immediately in the crowd, which was clamorous, slow, and agitated by interminable bargains. The peasants examined the cows, went off, came back, always in great perplexity and fear of being cheated, never quite daring to decide, spying at the eye of the seller, trying ceaselessly to discover the tricks of the man and the defect in the beast.

The women, having placed their great baskets at their feet, had pulled out the poultry, which lay upon the ground. tied by the legs, with eyes scared, with combs scarlet.

They listened to propositions, maintaining the prices, with a dry manner, with an impassible face; or, suddenly, perhaps, deciding to take the lower price which was offered, they cried out to the customer, who was departing slowly:

"All right, I'll let you have them, Mâit' Anthime."

Then, little by little, the square became empty, and when the *Angelus* struck midday those who lived at a distance poured into the inns.

At Jourdain's the great room was filled with eaters, just as the vast court was filled with vehicles of every sort—wagons, gigs, char-à-bancs, tilburys, tilt-carts which have no name, yellow with mud, misshapen, pieced together, raising their shafts to heaven like two arms, or it may be with their nose in the dirt and their rear in the air.

Just opposite to where the diners were at table the huge fireplace, full of clear flame, threw a lively heat on the backs of those who sat along the right. Three spits were turning, loaded with chickens, with pigeons, and with joints of mutton; and a delectable odor of roast meat, and of gravy gushing over crisp brown skin, took wing from the hearth, kindled merriment, caused mouths to water.

All the aristocracy of the plough were eating there, at Maît' Jourdain's, the innkeeper's, a dealer in horses also, and a sharp fellow who had made a pretty penny in his day.

The dishes were passed round, were emptied, with jugs of yellow cider. Every one told of his affairs, of his purchases and his sales. They asked news about the crops. The weather was good for green stuffs, but a little wet for wheat.

All of a sudden the drum rolled in the court before the

house. Every one, except some of the most indifferent, was on his feet at once, and ran to the door, to the windows, with his mouth still full and his napkin in his hand.

When the public crier had finished his tattoo he called forth in a jerky voice, making his pauses out of time:

"Be it known to the inhabitants of Goderville, and in general to all—persons present at the market, that there has been lost this morning, on the Beuzeville road between—nine and ten o'clock, a pocket-book of black leather, containing five hundred francs and business papers. You are requested to return it—to the mayor's office, at once, or to Maître Fortuné Houlbrèque, of Manneville. There will be twenty francs reward."

Then the man departed. They heard once more at a distance the dull beatings of the drum and the faint voice of the crier.

Then they began to talk of this event, reckoning up the chances which Maître Houlbrèque had of finding or of not finding his pocket-book again.

And the meal went on.

They were finishing their coffee when the corporal of gendarmes appeared on the threshold.

He asked:

"Is Maître Hauchecorne, of Bréauté, here?"

Maître Hauchecorne, seated at the other end of the table, answered:

"Here I am."

And the corporal resumed:

"Maître Hauchecorne, will you have the kindness to come with me to the mayor's office? M. le Maire would like to speak to you."

The peasant, surprised and uneasy, gulped down his little glass of cognac, got up, and, even worse bent over than in the morning, since the first steps after a rest were always particularly difficult, started off, repeating:

"Here I am, here I am."

And he followed the corporal.

The mayor was waiting for him, seated in an arm-chair. He was the notary of the place, a tall, grave man of pompous speech.

"Maître Hauchecorne," said he, "this morning, on the Beuzeville road, you were seen to pick up the pocket-book lost by Maître Houlbrèque, of Manneville."

The countryman, speechless, regarded the mayor,

frightened already by this suspicion which rested on him he knew not why.

"I, I picked up that pocket-book?"

"Yes, you."

"I swear I didn't even know nothing about it at all."

"You were seen."

"They saw me, me? Who is that who saw me?"

"M. Malandain, the harness-maker."

Then the old man remembered, understood, and, reddening with anger:

"Ah, he saw me, did he, the rascal? He saw me picking up this string here, M'sieu' le Maire."

And, fumbling at the bottom of his pocket, he pulled out of it the little end of string.

But the mayor incredulously shook his head:

"You will not make me believe, Maître Hauchecorne, that M. Malandain, who is a man worthy of credit, has mistaken this string for a pocket-book."

The peasant, furious, raised his hand and spit as if to attest his good faith, repeating:

"For all that, it is the truth of the good God, the blessed truth, M'sieu' le Maire. There! on my soul and my salvation I repeat it."

The mayor continued:

"After having picked up the thing in question you even looked for some time in the mud to see if a piece of money had not dropped out of it."

The good man was suffocated with indignation and with fear:

"If they can say!—if they can say . . . such lies as that to slander an honest man! If they can say!—"

He might protest, he was not believed.

He was confronted with M. Malandain, who repeated and sustained his testimony. They abused one another for an hour. At his own request Maître Hauchecorne was searched. Nothing was found upon him.

At last, the mayor, much perplexed, sent him away, warning him that he would inform the public prosecutor, and ask for orders.

The news had spread. When he left the mayor's office, the old man was surrounded, interrogated with a curiosity which was serious or mocking as the case might be, but into which no indignation entered. And he began to tell the story of the string. They did not believe him. They laughed.

He passed on, button-holed by every one, himself button-holing his acquaintances, beginning over and over again his tale and his protestations, showing his pockets turned inside out to prove that he had nothing.

They said to him:

"You old rogue, *va!*"

And he grew angry, exasperated, feverish, in despair at not being believed, and always telling his story.

The night came. It was time to go home. He set out with three of his neighbors, to whom he pointed out the place where he had picked up the end of string; and all the way he talked of his adventure.

That evening he made the round in the village of Bréauté, so as to tell every one. He met only unbelievers.

He was ill of it all night long.

The next day, about one in the afternoon, Marius Paumelle, a farm hand of Maître Breton, the market-gardener at Ymauville, returned the pocket-book and its contents to Maître Houlbrèque, of Manneville.

This man said, indeed, that he had found it on the road; but not knowing how to read, he had carried it home and given it to his master.

The news spread to the environs. Maître Hauchecorne was informed. He put himself at once upon the go, and began to relate his story as completed by the *dénouement.* He triumphed.

"What grieved me," said he, "was not the thing itself, do you understand; but it was the lies. There's nothing does you so much harm as being in disgrace for lying."

All day he talked of his adventure, he told it on the roads to the people who passed; at the cabaret to the people who drank; and the next Sunday, when they came out of church. He even stopped strangers to tell them about it. He was easy, now, and yet something worried him without his knowing exactly what it was. People had a joking manner while they listened. They did not seem convinced. He seemed to feel their tittle-tattle behind his back.

On Tuesday of the next week he went to market at Goderville, prompted entirely by the need of telling his story.

Malandain, standing on his door-step, began to laugh as he saw him pass. Why?

He accosted a farmer of Criquetot, who did not let him finish, and, giving him a punch in the pit of his stomach, cried in his face: "Oh you great rogue, *va!*" Then turned his heel upon him.

Maître Hauchecorne remained speechless, and grew more and more uneasy. Why had they called him "great rogue"?

When seated at table in Jourdain's tavern he began again to explain the whole affair.

A horse-dealer of Montivilliers shouted at him:

"Get out, get out you old scamp; I know all about your string!"

Hauchecorne stammered:

"But since they found it again, the pocket-book!"

But the other continued:

"Hold your tongue, daddy; there's one who finds it and there's another who returns it. And no one the wiser."

The peasant was choked. He understood at last. They accused him of having had the pocket-book brought back by an accomplice, by a confederate.

He tried to protest. The whole table began to laugh.

He could not finish his dinner, and went away amid a chorus of jeers.

He went home, ashamed and indignant, choked with rage, with confusion, the more cast-down since from his Norman cunning, he was, perhaps, capable of having done what they accused him of, and even of boasting of it as a good trick. His innocence dimly seemed to him impossible to prove, his craftiness being so well known. And he felt himself struck to the heart by the injustice of the suspicion.

Then he began anew to tell of his adventure, lengthening his recital every day, each time adding new proofs, more energetic protestations, and more solemn oaths which he thought of, which he prepared in his hours of solitude, his mind being entirely occupied by the story of the string. The more complicated his defence, the more artful his arguments, the less he was believed.

"Those are liars' proofs," they said behind his back.

He felt this; it preyed upon his heart. He exhausted himself in useless efforts.

He was visibly wasting away.

The jokers now made him tell the story of "The Piece

of String" to amuse them, just as you make a soldier who has been on a campaign tell his story of the battle. His mind, struck at the root, grew weak.

About the end of December he took to his bed.

He died early in January, and, in the delirium of the death-agony, he protested his innocence, repeating:

"A little bit of string—a little bit of string—see, here it is, M'sieu' le Maire."

Now we can consider how Maupassant tells his story:

The opening scene provides the setting, the crowded market-day in Goderville. We are given a panoramic view of hard-working peasant farmers (even "deformed" by their work), arriving to trade cattle and poultry. It is a day on which each man tries to get the better of another, each with a "fear of being cheated," and, as he haggles over prices, "trying ceaselessly to discover the tricks of the man and the defect in the beast." It is a world of poor, suspicious people, perhaps even deformed mentally by their suspicions. We are thus prepared for what follows in the story. A man is trying to sell faith in himself to people who are accustomed to trusting no one. Since people tend to see in others what they themselves are, the story grows logically from the opening scene.

The focus narrows in on Maître Hauchecorne, the leading character. He is the one who appears in all the scenes, is most affected by the action of the story, and causes the events to happen. His act of picking up a piece of string sets off the chain of events. In opposition to him we have two important minor characters. Maître Malandain, the harness-maker, who misinterprets Hauchecorne's act of picking up the string and thus introduces the conflict to the story. His misinterpretation, combined with his feeling of "malice" toward Hauchecorne, makes him willing to supply the latter's name to the mayor when the pocket-book disappears. The mayor, another minor character, chooses to believe Malandain's false version of what happened because the latter is "a man worthy of credit."

In unfolding his story, Maupassant adopts an omniscient point of view; he becomes a disembodied voice that tells the story. He can then know everything about his characters, past and present, including what they think. He can comment on, and so interpret, the meanings of their actions. He can give a broad view of the crowd, yet zoom in on a piece of string. If he had taken a more restricted point of view (setting himself up, for example, as a character in the town), his problems in telling the story would have differed greatly.

When Maupassant chooses the broadest point of view, we know that much of the story will be told (summarized), as opposed to being acted out (dramatized). Although the scene in the mayor's office is dramatized, even in this scene the author's voice is interpreting for the reader. The mayor, we are told, is a "man of pompous speech." And Hauchecorne "raised his hand and spit as if to attest his good faith." We can see the dramatic action of the raised hand and spit; the rest of the sentence is the author's voice, giving us the meaning.

When Maupassant says, "Maître Hauchecorne, economical, like all true Normans, reflected that everything was worth picking up which could be of any use; and he stooped down—but painfully, because he suffered from rheumatism," he is again allowing his own voice to interpret the action. We are *told* that Hauchecorne is "economical," that he believes "that everything was worth picking up which could be of any use," that it is painful for Hauchecorne to stoop "because he suffered from rheumatism." The author, then, is not limiting himself to what might be seen and heard by an observer on the scene. Some of the story is told dramatically (what can be seen and heard); some of it is summarized. The distinction is between showing and telling. Maupassant shifts from one to the other.

In arranging the plot, Maupassant sets up a cause-and-effect relation. Because it is the market-day, Hauchecorne has come to town. Because he is "economical," he picks up the string. Because he is seen by his enemy Malandain, he is reported as having found the pocket-book. Because no one believes his story, he dies. E. M. Forster, writing in *Aspects of the Novel*, says: "A plot is . . . a narrative of events, the emphasis falling on causality. 'The king died, and then the queen died' is a story. 'The king died, and then the queen died of grief' is a plot. The time-sequence is preserved, but the sense of causality overshadows it." In Maupassant's story we find out why Hauchecorne died, and the events are related in causal sequence.

The story possibly has a flaw in the credibility of its characterizations. We can accept Hauchecorne's picking up the string, and we can accept Malandain's "malice" because, as Maupassant tells us, "they had once had a quarrel about a halter." It is more difficult, however, to accept the fact that no one will believe Hauchecorne's story. The justification for this disbelief is Maupassant's saying of Hauchecorne:

> He went home, ashamed and indignant, choked with rage, with confusion, the more cast-down since from his Norman cunning, he was, perhaps, capable of having done what they accused him of, and even of boasting of it as a good trick. His innocence dimly seemed to him impossible to prove, his craftiness being so well known. And he felt himself struck to the heart by the injustice of the suspicion.

In this last quotation, note the word *perhaps.* Is he or is he not "cunning"? In the answer to the question lies our belief in the story. Later, the author moves into Hauchecorne's mind ("seemed to him"), and here Hauchecorne seems to be admitting his own "craftiness." At any rate, we are asked to accept the author's word as he interprets the character of Hauchecorne in this summarizing paragraph: he has "Norman cunning" and "was, perhaps, capable of having done what they accused him of, and even boasting of it as a good trick." Without this paragraph we would not understand why his word is less esteemed than that of Malandain.

In a good story the action usually grows out of some major characteristic of the person involved. One could argue here that the story grows out of Hauchecorne's being "economical." But his "cunning" is a stronger cause for his downfall, and this last characteristic is introduced by the author from outside the action of the story.

By summarizing, an author can speed up the telling of his story; depicting a scene in detail takes time. Maupassant begins with a generalized summary of the crowd, moving to specific action as the cart "with two men on the seat" moves by. Then we see Hauchecorne pick up the string. We see and hear the action as the drum rolls and the public crier announces the loss of the pocket-book, followed quickly by the visit of the gendarme.

The story slows as we see and hear the scene in the mayor's

office, when Hauchecorne pleads his innocence. This is a key scene, and we can assume that Hauchecorne's subsequent, summarized attempts to convince others of his innocence resemble his conversation with the mayor. But the attempts end in "You old rogue, *va*."

After the pocket-book is found, each of Hauchecorne's encounters on his return to Goderville is sketched quickly; all are variations on the talk with the mayor, and Hauchecorne dies repeating what he had said to that official.

Finally, we should look at the meaning of the story—its theme. In a good story an author is certainly dealing with a specific act in a particular place, but a story lasts and is reread if it also carries a profound truth about human behavior. We could argue here that Maupassant's story shows that simple acts may, in some circumstances, be misunderstood.

If we look back at the paragraph from the story quoted above, we might say that Maupassant is suggesting his theme in the sentence "His innocence dimly seemed to him impossible to prove, his craftiness being so well known." Since an author uses his material to express some general statement about life, we might draw a more universal truth from the story. We could say that Maupassant's theme is that people will believe the worst of those who have bad reputations.

POINT OF VIEW

Point of view is a term used to describe the way the actions of a story are reported to the reader. It is the perspective of the narrator toward the materials of the story that determines what information the reader is given, in what order, with what emphasis, and in what tone.

The author writes the story, but he often introduces a narrator who tells it. The reader must distinguish between the author of the story and the narrator's voice that *tells* the story. As a story begins, the words we see or "hear" are given to us by a "voice" that describes what happens. A narrator is never wholly objective, even if he seems to be; that is, he does not completely omit his own feelings or attitudes toward what is happening. The reader must be aware of the relationship of the narrator to the story. On one hand the voice may be that of a seemingly objective narrator who allows the story to act itself out and makes no comments on the action. We hear voices within the story and see actions, but we must make our own inferences about what the characters are like. On the other hand, the narrator may refer to himself as "I," and the story may be about him, in which case his point of view will of course be subjective; or he may be an "active" observer of the action, commenting on what he sees and offering opinions that affect the reader's interpretations of the action.

Even when the narrator's attitude is not obvious, he must see the action from a particular vantage point, just as he would take a particular stance with a camera. He must select some things and, equally important, omit others. He may comment, in summarizing statements, on the meaning of the action. In such ways he takes a mental attitude toward his material, approving and disapproving selectively. The connotation of his diction may give us clues to his intent.

We should also note the vantage point of the narrator to determine his distance in time and space from the events being described. The idea of recalling an event from the past (variations of "Once upon a time . . .") puts the narrator at some distance. A stance that takes the reader into the event in the present (when we see and hear the event from close up) appears more immediate and more concrete and may therefore more fully involve the reader's belief in the fact that something is truly happening.

Two general types of narrators are commonly designated. The narrator can be a disembodied voice, speaking from an omniscient point of view; that is, he can know everything. He can tell us what characters think, what they do when they are alone, and he can follow one character and then another. He can go backward or forward in time. Such a narrator is called an omniscient narrator.

By setting up a more restricted focus, the author may have his story told by a narrator who appears in the story, calls himself "I," and becomes a major character, a minor character, or merely an observer. This last device will restrict the narrator in what he can see and know. A common device is to create a narrator who does not understand what is going on although the reader eventually will. Here we speak of a limited narrator.

Questions on Point of View

Who is telling the story? What is his relation to the action? Does he take part in the action? If so, is he the main character or a minor character? Or is he a disembodied voice? How is the unfolding of the story limited? How much does the narrator know of the meaning of the events? About what the characters are thinking? About each character? What do we learn about the narrator by the way that he reports the action?

From what place and time does the narrator "see" the action? Are we close to the action, watching it happen; or is it being recalled as something that happened in the past? What proportion of the story is "acted out"? How much is summarized as expository narrative? What offstage events are merely told to us?

In what order are the events narrated? Do they follow a chronological sequence? Are there flashbacks into the past? If so, how are the interruptions related to the structure of the story?

Does the narrator judge the action? Can we trust his judgment? In what ways does the narrator take sides; that is, what opinions does he express about the characters or the action? How does he express those opinions: through the connotations of descriptive words, by direct summary, or by what the characters say and do? Or is the story told objectively, as far as possible? Is it merely acted out without the intrusion of judgments by the narrator?

On what character is the narrator focusing? How does he keep the focus on that character? Do some characters in the story see things differently from the way the narrator does?

How is the point of view of the narration related to the main intent of the story?

PLOT

Plot is the action of the story and is made up of a series of related episodes and incidents that carry the story through from a conflict to a conclusion. The characters ordinarily act out the major events, and those events are usually connected by cause-and-effect relationships. The author presents the action and gives it meaning by what he chooses to include or exclude. As with point of view, selection is of the utmost importance. In a newspaper account of an episode, we are given only the events, what happened. If we read a story based on the same events, we learn *why* they happened, what the motivation was.

At the beginning, when we enter imaginatively into the world of the story, we are given the exposition, an explanation of where and when the action is taking place and who the actors are. We are told what the situation is at the opening moment. If it is necessary, we are told something of the past. Sometimes we are told directly by the voice of the narrator; sometimes by one of the characters; sometimes through clues in the setting. Often we are given the information in the first few paragraphs, or it may be strung out over several pages. Or pertinent information may be withheld for a purpose that we will understand as the story develops.

The structure of the plot is based on the motivation, why something happened as it did. For this reason the outcome must be logical; it must grow out of the action. If the ending comes as a surprise, we should check to see whether we have missed some hints or foreshadowings of where the story was going. If the hints are not there, to that extent the story is a failure. It is in life that we continually see unexplained actions, and do not always understand why people act as they do. In art, life is explained; the writer takes us into the minds of the characters. Motivation helps to make us believe that something is really happening by making it likely or logical.

The actions of the plot must have signifiance: they should cause the leading character to react to them, or he should cause the actions to occur. There must be an interplay, a conflict, between the plot and the character. In a story in which the action is more important (an adventure or detective story, for example), the character reacts to what happens. In a story in which characterization is more important, the character causes much of the action, which grows out of the kind of person he is.

A significant action, then, will produce conflict. A leading character wants something, but something else stands in his way of getting it. The conflict usually takes one of three forms: it may be between the leading character and one or more of the actors in the story; it may be largely a struggle of a person with himself; or it may be the struggle of a person against fate or circumstance. But often these kinds of conflict overlap.

Because of the conflict, we also have suspense. The early part of a story is usually the building up of the complication, the problem that must be solved. We read on to find out what will happen.

The complication ends at the point where the leading character's position changes, where he makes his decision or has it made for him. We call this point where we can see how the story will come out the climax: it is the resolution of the complication.

A plot, then, usually has three main parts: the motivation; the main action, or climax; and the results of that action, or dénouement (a French word meaning *untying*). The third of these parts, the result, is often played down or merely suggested in short stories, leaving us to draw our own inferences.

A plot is often based on the reversal of a situation. A character may learn something about himself or his situation that he did not know before. This self-knowledge may come to him as a burden if he finds himself defeated, or as a relief if he is a winner; he may move from satisfaction to frustration or from frustration to satisfaction. The action of the story may cause a loss of innocence when a person who does not suspect its existence discovers evil in a situation. Or the plot may enlighten the character, changing his perception from a false to a true view of a situation.

This last type of reversal, when a result is the opposite of what might be expected or appropriate, where reality contradicts appearance, is known as dramatic irony. The situation turns out to be the reverse of what the character thought it was; what is expected is contradicted by what actually happens. In a short story, the scene last presented may be in ironic contrast to an earlier one. In such a contrast, the reader may understand the situation more fully than does the character taking part in the action.

Questions on Plot

As you read the story and write about the plot, the following questions will help you to see how the plot works.

Where and when is the action taking place? What is the situation as the story begins? What, if anything, are we told about the past? Where and how are these details given? Are they told directly or implied? At the end of the opening scene, what questions about the outcome are we left with?

What are the main events of the story? What is the purpose of each scene? What is the conflict, the problem to be solved? What are the opposing forces: Is the struggle mainly one of man against man, of man against himself, or of man against fate and circumstance? Are there minor conflicts within the scenes that lead up to the climax? Where is the climax of the story? How is it resolved? What is the effect of the major decision on the events and the position of the leading character?

How is the plot directed—by the events, by a character, or by both? Does the story proceed chronologically, or are there flashbacks? Does the ending grow logically out of the events? What foreshadowing is used?

Is the movement of the plot toward a reversal in the leading character's condition? If so, what is the nature of the reversal? Is it ironic? What span of time is covered by the events in the story? Where has the author summarized the action? Where has he dramatized it? Why did he make his choices between telling and showing?

CHARACTERIZATION

A main goal of many stories is to reveal something about a character's personality. What a person is like is most apparent in moments of stress or conflict, when he must react to a situation that is forced on him or that he creates. Consequently, to create an interesting story, a writer chooses a significant conflict in the life of his main character. He prepares us for the key moment by beginning to define the character; in the key moment we learn much more.

An author has several methods of revealing character. Ordinarily action and dialogue are the chief methods. The person acts or speaks, and the reader draws a conclusion. This is called the dramatic method, because action and speech are what we see on a stage, or in life. The reader expresses his conclusion with a general or characterizing term: cruel, brave, dishonest, hypocritical, or whatever fits the evidence. When we add up the terms that we can apply to the character, we have completed what is called a characterization. The author creates his character by giving us the evidence; we make our characterization by drawing our own conclusions from that evidence. To read well enough to draw inferences from a story takes experience in living, in seeing the relation between what people do and what they are like. But reading is also a way of expanding our experience with people; the more we read, the more possible it is that we will become better judges of what people are really like.

To delineate a characterization, we must first clarify who the main character is, on whom the story is focusing. One test is that he will appear in all, or most, scenes. He makes the key decision and causes the action to happen; or he is the one to whom something happens, mentally or physically.

The author's methods of characterizing may be apparent or subtle. The simplest way of characterizing is just by telling: "John is honest"; but few writers now would consider using so easy a method. They prefer showing to telling. A hero may be put in a scene in which we learn his chief characteristic; then, in a similar but more important scene, that same characteristic may reappear. A writer will often be subtle: a jaw tightens, or a seemingly chance remark takes on great significance. The degree of subtlety largely depends on what is left to the reader's inference. Our experience with movies and television has made us aware of the method: hints have replaced explanations. Red, roughened hands may tell us something about a woman, as will soft hands and long fingernails. A torn handkerchief can represent stress.

The character's name may be suggestive. A few extreme examples can be illustrative. Thomas Gradgrind, says Dickens, was a man "of facts . . . ready to weigh and measure any parcel of human nature and tell you exactly what it comes to." Or consider names like Allworthy, Backbite, Sharp, Dartle, or Pecksniff; they predispose us to take a particular attitude toward a person. Sometimes a name (Ahab or Ishmael) will be an allusion to a story that we are likely to know or that we can look up; this causes us to expect the person to have some of the characteristics of the person in that story (in this case, of their Biblical prototypes).

The device of giving characters names appropriate to their natures or their situations has a long history and continues with, for example, Benet's Jabez Stone, in "The Devil and Daniel Webster," Steinbeck's cowboy Billy Buck, in "The Red Pony," Sherwood Anderson's farmer Thomas Butterworth, a minor character in "The Egg," and Bret Harte's strong man Oakhurst, in "The Outcasts of Poker Flat."

Descriptions of physical appearance may tell us something about a person. In "Bartleby the Scrivener" Melville says, "Nippers . . . was a whiskered, sallow, . . . rather piratical-looking young man of about five and twenty. . . . indigestion seemed betokened in an occasional nervous testiness and grinning irritability, causing the teeth to audibly grind together. . . ." Or the author's comments may deal with a man's psychological state. Maupassant, as we saw in "The Piece of String," comments on his main character, "And he grew angry, exasperated, feverish, in despair at not being believed, and always telling his story."

An outward action can express an inward thought. What that thought is we can infer from the action, sometimes from the setting, often from a symbol that comes into prominence—or from a failure to act, from silence. In Katherine Mansfield's "The Fly," a retired worker calls on his former boss and friend, who has spent much of his time ostensibly mourning for his son, killed a few years before in war. When the visitor mentions that "the girls" in his family have just returned from Belgium and had happened across the son's grave, ". . . the boss made no reply. Only a quiver in his eyelids showed that he had heard." Though the two old friends had been carrying on a normal conversation, the mention of the son causes the boss to stop talking, but the visitor goes on chatting, unaware of what has happened. When the visitor leaves, the rest of the story deals with the boss's resolution of his thoughts toward his son's death.

When, in Poe's "The Cask of Amontillado," Montresor is about to get revenge for a "thousand injuries" by sealing Fortunato into a wall, Montresor discusses his family seal. Fortunato, who thinks he has come to sample a fine wine, asks,

"I forget your arms."

"A huge human foot d'or, in a field azure; the foot crushes a serpent rampant whose fangs are imbedded in the heel."

"And the motto?"

"Nemo me impune lacessit." [Nobody provokes me without punishment.] Here is an example of a person's thoughts revealed through the symbolism of the coat of arms. Montresor will kill Fortunato, and the motto has shown us why. Poe used the setting to comment on a person's mind in "The Fall of the House of Usher." Roderick Usher suffers from "nervous agitation"; after his mind breaks completely, a fissure appears "from the roof of the building, in a zigzag direction, to the base," and the house collapses.

Another method of characterizing is the use of a minor character to give us information through his interaction with the main character. What he says must be examined for motive and reliability, however. Can we trust what the minor character says? Have we examined what he knows, and on what he bases his judgment? The reader must marshal all the facts that he has been given throughout the story to come to a valid conclusion.

A minor character can be used as a contrast or parallel to the main character. In Conrad's "The Secret Sharer," a young captain who has just taken command of a ship wonders whether he will be able to carry out his duty. As the captain walks alone on the deck of the anchored ship, a man swims to its side and is helped aboard. He turns out to be the captain's double and is kept hidden in the captain's cabin. It becomes clear that he represents the captain's other self, his doubts. As the two talk, we learn that Leggatt, the visitor, has failed in an emergency situation, thus reflecting what the captain thinks may happen to him. When the captain gets rid of the man Leggatt, his other self, he casts off his doubts and is ready to command his ship.

A minor character may represent an opposing characteristic or situation, and thereby help to precipitate the conflict. In Frank O'Connor's "Guests of the Nation," which you will read later in this section, an Irish soldier is reluctant to kill two prisoner-friends when he is ordered to do so. The leader of the small group of soldiers, who must carry out the order to kill the prisoners, feels no ethical dilemma. The clash of the ideas represented by these two men becomes the central interest of the story. Such a minor character as the group leader can show us much of what a major character is like by acting as a foil, a contrast to show the qualities of another person.

In fiction we can know more about a character than we could if he were real. We can know what he does when he is alone, what he thinks, what others think of him, and what the author's attitude is toward him. We may learn that attitude from the author's tone—serious, humorous, derisive—in describing him. The author may choose descriptive words that convey his attitude through what they connote. Most important, he is putting his character under a spotlight and focusing on speeches and actions that we might miss in ordinary life.

As we put together a characterization of a person, we need to explain his motivation. Why did he do that? Did he make his own decision, or was it forced on him by the circumstances? As we pointed out earlier, the circumstances of the plot will bear on a person's actions, but so will his psychological makeup, his beliefs, his environment, and any pressure brought by minor characters.

Another important consideration in making a characterization is to consider how the person responds to the results of his actions, whether he has learned anything, and whether he is changed by his experience.

Questions on Characterization

Who is the leading character? What do we learn about him from what he says, does, or thinks? From his environment and his reaction to it? From his interaction with minor characters? Is his name significant?

What are the minor characters like? How do they interact with the major character? Are they merely furthering the plot or are they helping to characterize the main character? Is any minor character used as a parallel to the main character?

What problem does the leading character face early in the story? How does he react to it? What is the most important action of the main character? Why did he take this action? How much was he influenced by fate and circumstances? By his environment? By his moral or psychological makeup? How does his situation at the end differ from what is was at the beginning? What did he learn about himself? Does he change in the course of the story?

Does the character's behavior grow out of the circumstances? Given the kind of person he is, could he have acted in a different way at the moment of crisis? Does he overcome his problem or is he defeated by it?

Is the meaning of the story clear to the main character or only to the reader? How much does the character learn about the truth of his situation? Does the reader know more? Has the author tried to present a realistic character, one true to life as we know it, or has he deliberately avoided realism?

What methods does the author use in the characterization? Does he comment directly? Does he expect the reader to infer a characterization from what the character does? Is the character's physical appearance part of the characterization? Are we told what he thinks, or are his thoughts suggested by actions, by the setting, or by symbols? What is the author's attitude toward the character?

SETTING

As a story begins, it must be located in some place at some time. But the setting can give us much more than this basic information. We must assume that the setting is related to the total effect of the story; that it is somehow connected to the action. The problem is to work out the possible connections.

An author may create a setting by telling us through direct descriptive statements. A character in the story may give us the information by what he says or by what he sees. The setting may be described in one section of a story, or it may be implied by hints throughout the scenes.

The most obvious purpose of the setting is to create an illusion of reality, to take us into a recognizable world. As we read the author's words, we project in our minds the scene in which the action is taking place. If the world seems "real," we are more likely to be drawn into believing the story. How much of the scene the author creates by detailing description and how much by mere suggestion will vary with the author's purpose. He is like a painter: he may meticulously draw out the details so that they are sharply defined, or he may merely suggest shapes and forms, leaving the details to the reader's imagination. We can assume that his manner is one of deliberate choice.

On another level the setting may enhance the characterization. The room in which a person lives can tell us something about him; a street depicts one aspect of his environment. We can learn whether he is rich or poor, proud or depressed, trapped or free. The setting may help in causing and determining the conflict. One way of thinking about such matters is to consider whether a change in the setting would change the action of the plot.

A setting can also be used to establish the mood of the story. Through the images and diction used in describing the setting, the author can affect our emotional attitude by drawing on our own experience. His use of light and dark can move us in different ways, just as a sunlit day may cheer us up while a gray day may depress us. His use of colors—bright reds and yellows as opposed to browns and purples—will help to manipulate our feelings. The seasons of the year may evoke different emotions, as will the shapes painted for us: a snow storm on a jagged mountain will move us differently from spring flowers on a green hill. A setting can suggest sounds or silence: different kinds of winds, crashing waves, bubbling brooks, the call of a thrush, a deep, quiet forest, or a soundless mountain top.

Our emotions respond to these stimuli because of our previous experiences; a particular word or phrase will evoke associations from the past. All the associations and overtones a word carries, in addition to its explicit meaning, embody its connotation, and a good writer will use connotation effectively to influence his reader. Recall, for example, how we react to the images that make up a particular advertisement for an automobile or a cigarette. An author, too, uses images—concrete words that appeal to our senses, remind us of our past, and affect our emotions. His diction, his choice of words, and what the words connote, will help to establish a mood. He may refer to a torrent of rain or describe a shower; a wind may cause trees to groan or leaves to dance. If we mentally underline words used for their connotative value, we can determine the mood of the setting.

We must be particularly aware of changes in the setting: the rising or setting of the sun, the beginning of a storm, a crash of thunder. They may reflect some change in the fortunes of the character. Rather than tell you what a person is thinking, the author may reflect it in what he chooses to describe at the time or in what the character sees.

The setting may also be a metaphoric statement; that is, it may provide a comparison with the plight of the person in the story. A rising or setting sun could symbolize the rise or fall in a person's fortunes. A broad expanse of landscape might emphasize the loneliness or isolation of a character, or a storm suggest the turbulence in his mind.

A setting may be used ironically, as a contrast to the state of an actor in a scene. What seems to be may not be the real situation. A particular picture on a wall may suggest an ironic contrast to what is happening under it. A room suggesting great wealth and stability could be the setting for the revelation of instability in a character. A church might be the scene of a murder.

Closely related to the metaphoric use of setting is the symbolic use of setting: particular inanimate objects may take on symbolic meaning; they may stand for abstract ideas. The chopping down of an orchard on an estate to build small houses, as in Chekhov's *The Cherry Orchard,* may symbolize the ending of a way of life, as the common people take over from the aristocracy. A swimming pool, which at one point is a symbol of success, may come to represent the destructive quality of a particular kind of life when the story ends with the owner dead in the pool, as in F. Scott Fitzgerald's *The Great Gatsby*.

Whatever parts of the setting are pointed out should be examined carefully for their relation to the meaning of the action. Chekhov once reminded writers that if early in a story they point out a gun on a wall, the gun must go off before the story ends. Nothing in a literary work should be irrelevant; everything should fit the purpose of the work.

Questions on Setting

What is the time and place of the story? In how much detail is the setting described? Is the setting realistic, or has the author deliberately avoided a particular time and place?

How much does the setting tell us about the people in the story? Are the characters affected by the setting? Does the setting help to establish the conflict? Does it affect the resolution of the conflict?

What effect does the setting have on the mood of the story? What devices are used to establish the mood—light or dark, color, weather, season of the year, the massing of shapes, sound or silence? What specific images affect the emotional reaction to the story?

Does the setting or the mood shift? How does the shift relate to the action? What elements in the setting reflect what a person is thinking or what is happening to him at that point in the story? Is the setting ever used metaphorically? Is it used as an ironic comment on the action? Does anything in the setting take on symbolic meaning? If so, what does it symbolize?

THEME

The theme of a work of literature is the main idea, the abstract statement of what the work means, its significance. Sometimes we may find a statement of a theme written into the work; more often the reader has to infer the theme by stating how the parts of the story are related to a central meaning. As the story unfolds, the theme is acted out.

The statement of what a story means can take the form of a sentence or a paragraph, depending on the complexity of the story. The statement should be a general one, applying not only to the story, but also showing its relation to life.

A writer is never merely reporting what happens, as we would see episodes happen in life. He is interpreting his material, giving it meaning by the way that he organizes his point of view, plot, characters, and setting. We assume, then, that all parts of the story are related to a central meaning, or theme. And that theme is an insight into human existence perhaps offering a complex view of what life is about.

How do we find the theme? You probably know the story of the shepherd who twice cried, "Wolf!" and thought it a great joke when help arrived and there was no wolf. When a wolf really did attack his flock, the shepherd's cries went unanswered. This story, then, illustrates the idea that people fooled twice may not respond a third time, or "don't call for help unless you need it." In this instance, we found the theme by seeing a relationship between the various scenes in the story.

Most often, the theme is not stated outright in the work; the reader must derive from the action a general theme that will take into account the way all the elements of the story relate to a wider statement or idea.

Sometimes the theme is suggested by what happens to a character. In "Paul's Case," by Willa Cather, a boy finds that death is the only ending for one who will accept no social responsibilities. Or it may be found in the central conflict. In W. W. Jacobs' "The Monkey's Paw," a man finds that he cannot control fate by supernatural means. Often we will find a repeated, significant phrase that becomes a subtheme (often called a motif or thematic statement) that runs through the story. In Katherine Mansfield's "A Cup of Tea," the word *pretty* is repeated several times; at the end it appears in a question, "Philip, am I *pretty?*" Its use reinforces the insecurity of the major character.

A title may help in determining the theme. Conrad's title "Heart of Darkness" refers to the center of Africa, the literal setting of the climax of the story. But it also means the dark center of the human soul that lives without the restraints of civilized behavior.

Do not look in stories for simple morals like Things will always get better or Good will always triumph over evil. A writer worth reading demonstrates that life is more complex than such simple statements would indicate, and he gives the intelligent reader something to think about. Rather than search for a moral, we do draw a theme, or unifying idea, from a literary work. But a good story does not merely illustrate a theme; it modifies the theme by showing the complexity of the idea.

Questions on Theme

What is the theme of the work? Is the theme stated in the work itself or must the reader infer it from the action? Is the theme suggested by the relationship between the scenes? By a change that takes place in the main character? By the conflict in the story? Are there motifs that help to clarify the theme?

WRITING ABOUT A SHORT STORY

Some of the points so far discussed can be illustrated by the following story "Guests of the Nation," by Frank O'Connor (first published in 1931). After you have read the story we will discuss how to write a paper about it.

GUESTS OF THE NATION

Frank O'Connor

At dusk the big Englishman, Belcher, would shift his long legs out of the ashes and say "Well, chums, what about it?" and Noble or me would say "All right, chum" (for we had picked up some of their curious expressions), and the little Englishman, Hawkins, would light the lamp and bring out the cards. Sometimes Jeremiah Donovan would come up and supervise the game and get exicted over Hawkins's cards, which he always played badly, and shout at him as if he was one of our own "Ah, you divil, you, why didn't you play the tray?"

But ordinarily Jeremiah was a sober and contented poor devil like the big Englishman, Belcher, and was looked up to only because he was a fair hand at documents, though he was slow enough even with them. He wore a small cloth hat and big gaiters over his long pants, and you seldom saw him with his hands out of his pockets. He reddened when you talked to him, tilting from toe to heel and back, and looking down all the time at his big farmer's feet. Noble and me used to make fun of his broad accent, because we were from the town.

I couldn't at the time see the point of me and Noble guarding Belcher and Hawkins at all, for it was my belief that you could have planted that pair down anywhere from this to Claregalway and they'd have taken root there like a native weed. I never in my short experience seen two men to take to the country as they did.

They were handed on to us by the Second Battalion when the search for them became too hot, and Noble and myself, being young, took over with a natural feeling of responsibility, but Hawkins made us look like fools when he showed that he knew the country better than we did.

"You're the bloke they calls Bonaparte," he says to me. "Mary Brigid O'Connell told me to ask you what you done with the pair of her brother's socks you borrowed."

For it seemed, as they explained it, that the Second used to have little evenings, and some of the girls of the neighbourhood turned in, and, seeing they were such decent chaps, our fellows couldn't leave the two Englishmen out of them. Hawkins learned to dance "The Walls of Limerick," "The Siege of Ennis," and "The Waves of Tory" as well as any of them, though, naturally, he couldn't return the compliment, because our lads at that time did not dance foreign dances on principle.

So whatever privileges Belcher and Hawkins had with the Second they just naturally took with us, and after the first day or two we gave up all pretence of keeping a close eye on them. Not that they could have got far, for they had accents you could cut with a knife and wore khaki tunics and overcoats with civilian pants and boots. But it's my belief that they never had any idea of escaping and were quite content to be where they were.

It was a treat to see how Belcher got off with the old woman of the house where we were staying. She was a great warrant to scold, and cranky even with us, but before ever she had a chance of giving our guests, as I may call them, a lick of her tongue, Belcher had made her his friend for life. She was breaking sticks, and Belcher, who hadn't been more than ten minutes in the house, jumped up from his seat and went over to her.

"Allow me, madam," he says, smiling his queer little smile, "please allow me"; and he takes the bloody hatchet. She was struck too paralytic to speak, and after that, Belcher would be at her heels, carrying a bucket, a basket, or a load of turf, as the case might be. As Noble said, he got into looking before she leapt, and hot water, or any little thing she wanted, Belcher would have it ready for her. For such a huge man (and though I am five foot ten myself I had to look up at him) he had an uncommon shortness—or should I say lack?—of speech. It took us some time to get used to him, walking in and out, like a ghost, without a word. Especially because Hawkins talked enough for a platoon, it was strange to hear big Belcher with his toes in the ashes come out with a solitary "Excuse me, chum," or "That's right, chum." His one and only passion was cards, and I will say for him that he was a good card-player. He could have fleeced myself and Noble, but whatever we lost to him Hawkins lost to us, and Hawkins played with the money Belcher gave him.

Hawkins lost to us because he had too much old gab, and we probably lost to Belcher for the same reason. Hawkins and Noble would spit at one another about religion into the early hours of the morning, and Hawkins worried the soul out of Noble, whose brother was a priest, with a string of questions that would puzzle a cardinal. To make it worse, even in treating of holy subjects, Hawkins had a deplorable tongue. I never in all my career met a man who could mix such a variety of cursing and bad language into an argument. He was a terrible man, and a fright to argue. He never did a stroke of work, and when he had no one else to talk to, he got stuck in the old woman.

He met his match in her, for one day when he tried to get her to complain profanely of the drought, she gave him a great come-down by blaming it entirely on Jupiter Pluvius (a deity neither Hawkins nor I had ever heard of, though Noble said that among the pagans it was believed that he had something to do with the rain). Another day he was swearing at the capitalists for starting the German war when the old lady laid down her iron, puckered up her little crab's mouth, and said: "Mr. Hawkins, you can say what you like about the war, and think you'll deceive me because I'm only a simple poor countrywoman, but I know what started the war. It was the Italian Count that stole the heathen divinity out of the temple in Japan. Believe me, Mr. Hawkins, nothing but sorrow and want can follow the people that disturb the hidden powers."

A queer old girl, all right.

II

We had our tea one evening, and Hawkins lit the lamp and we all sat into cards. Jeremiah Donovan came in too, and sat down and watched us for a while, and it suddenly struck me that he had no great love for the two Englishmen. It came as a great surprise to me, because I hadn't noticed anything about him before.

Late in the evening a really terrible argument blew up between Hawkins and Noble, about capitalists and priests and love of your country.

"The capitalists," says Hawkins with an angry gulp, "pays the priests to tell you about the next world so as you won't notice what the bastards are up to in this."

"Nonsense, man!" says Noble, losing his temper. "Before ever a capitalist was thought of, people believed in the next world."

Hawkins stood up as though he was preaching a sermon.

"Oh, they did, did they?" he says with a sneer. "They believed all the things you believe, isn't that what you mean? And you believe that God created Adam, and Adam created Shem, and Shem created Jehoshophat. You believe all that silly old fairytale about Eve and Eden and the apple. Well, listen to me, chum. If you're entitled to hold a silly belief like that, I'm entitled to hold my silly belief—which is that the first thing your God created was a bleeding capitalist, with morality and Rolls-Royce complete. Am I right, chum?" he says to Belcher.

"You're right, chum," says Belcher with his amused smile, and got up from the table to stretch his long legs into the fire and stroke his moustache. So, seeing that Jeremiah Donovan was going, and that there was no knowing when the argument about religion would be over, I went out with him. We strolled down to the village together, and then he stopped and started blushing and mumbling and saying I ought to be behind, keeping guard on the prisoners. I didn't like the tone he took with me, and anyway I was bored with life in the cottage, so I replied by asking him what the hell we wanted guarding them at all for. I told him I'd talked it over with Noble, and that we'd both rather be out with a fighting column.

"What use are those fellows to us?" says I.

He looked at me in surprise and said: "I thought you knew we were keeping them as hostages."

"Hostages?" I said.

"The enemy have prisoners belonging to us," he says, "and now they're talking of shooting them. If they shoot our prisoners, we'll shoot theirs."

"Shoot them?" I said.

"What else did you think we were keeping them for?" he says.

"Wasn't it very unforeseen of you not to warn Noble and myself of that in the beginning?" I said.

"How was it?" says he. "You might have known it."

"We couldn't know it, Jeremiah Donovan," says I. "How could we when they were on our hands so long?"

"The enemy have our prisoners as long and longer," says he.

"That's not the same thing at all," says I.

"What difference is there?" says he.

I couldn't tell him, because I knew he wouldn't understand. If it was only an old dog that was going to the vet's, you'd try and not get too fond of him, but Jeremiah Donovan wasn't a man that would ever be in danger of that.

"And when is this thing going to be decided?" says I.

"We might hear tonight," he says. "Or tomorrow or the next day at latest. So if it's only hanging round here that's a trouble to you, you'll be free soon enough."

It wasn't the hanging round that was a trouble to me at all by this time. I had worse things to worry about. When I got back to the cottage the argument was still on. Hawkins was holding forth in his best style, maintaining that there was no next world, and Noble was maintaining that there was; but I could see that Hawkins had had the best of it.

"Do you know what, chum?" he was saying with a saucy smile. "I think you're just as big a bleeding unbeliever as I am. You say you believe in the next world, and you know just as much about the next world as I do, which is sweet damn-all. What's heaven? You don't know. Where's heaven? You don't know. You know sweet damn-all! I ask you again, do they wear wings?"

"Very well, then," says Noble, "they do. Is that enough for you? They do wear wings."

"Where do they get them, then? Who makes them? Have they a factory for wings? Have they a sort of store where you hands in your chit and takes your bleeding wings?"

"You're an impossible man to argue with," says Noble. "Now, listen to me—" And they were off again.

It was long after midnight when we locked up and went to bed. As I blew out the candle I told Noble what Jeremiah Donovan was after telling me. Noble took it very quietly. When we'd been in bed about an hour he asked me did I think we ought to tell the Englishmen. I didn't think we should, because it was more than likely that the English wouldn't shoot our men, and even if they did, the brigade officers, who were always up and down with the Second Battalion and knew the Englishmen well, wouldn't be likely to want them plugged. "I think so too," says Noble. "It would be great cruelty to put the wind up them now."

"It was very unforeseen of Jeremiah Donovan anyhow," says I.

It was next morning that we found it so hard to face Belcher and Hawkins. We went about the house all day scarcely saying a word. Belcher didn't seem to notice; he was stretched into the ashes as usual, with his usual look of waiting in quietness for something unforeseen to happen, but Hawkins noticed and put it down to Noble's being beaten in the argument of the night before.

"Why can't you take a discussion in the proper spirit?" he says severely. "You and your Adam and Eve! I'm a Communist, that's what I am. Communist or anarchist, it all comes to much the same thing." And for hours he went round the house, muttering when the fit took him. "Adam and Eve! Adam and Eve! Nothing better to do with their time than picking bleeding apples!"

III

I don't know how we got through that day, but I was very glad when it was over, the tea things were cleared away, and Belcher said in his peaceable way: "Well, chums, what about it?" We sat round the table and Hawkins took out the cards, and just then I heard Jeremiah Donovan's footstep on the path and a dark presentiment crossed my mind. I rose from the table and caught him before he reached the door.

"What do you want?" I asked.

"I want those two soldier friends of yours," he says, getting red.

"Is that the way, Jeremiah Donovan?" I asked.

"That's the way. There were four of our lads shot this morning, one of them a boy of sixteen."

"That's bad," I said.

At that moment Noble followed me out, and the three of us walked down the path together, talking in whispers. Feeney, the local intelligence officer, was standing by the gate.

"What are you going to do about it?" I asked Jeremiah Donovan.

"I want you and Noble to get them out; tell them they're being shifted again; that'll be the quietest way."

"Leave me out of that," says Noble under his breath.

Jeremiah Donovan looks at him hard.

"All right," he says. "You and Feeney get a few tools from the shed and dig a hole by the far end of the bog. Bonaparte and myself will be after you. Don't let anyone see you with the tools. I wouldn't like it to go beyond ourselves."

We saw Feeney and Noble go round to the shed and went in ourselves. I left Jeremiah Donovan to do the explanations. He told them that he had orders to send them back to the Second Battalion. Hawkins let out a mouthful of curses, and you could see that though Belcher didn't say anything, he was a bit upset too. The old woman was for having them stay in spite of us, and she didn't stop advising them until Jeremiah Donovan lost his temper and turned on her. He had a nasty temper, I noticed. It was pitch-dark in the cottage by this time, but no one thought of lighting the lamp, and in the darkness the two Englishmen fetched their topcoats and said good-bye to the old woman.

"Just as a man makes a home of a bleeding place, some bastard at headquarters thinks you're too cushy and shunts you off," says Hawkins, shaking her hand.

"A thousand thanks, madam," says Belcher. "A thousand thanks for everything"—as though he'd made it up.

We went round to the back of the house and down

towards the bog. It was only then that Jeremiah Donovan told them. He was shaking with excitement.

"There were four of our fellows shot in Cork this morning and now you're to be shot as a reprisal."

"What are you talking about?" snaps Hawkins. "It's bad enough being mucked about as we are without having to put up with your funny jokes."

"It isn't a joke," says Donovan. "I'm sorry, Hawkins, but it's true," and begins on the usual rigmarole about duty and how unpleasant it is.

I never noticed that people who talk a lot about duty find it much of a trouble to them.

"Oh, cut it out!" says Hawkins.

"Ask Bonaparte," says Donovan, seeing that Hawkins isn't taking him seriously. "Isn't it true, Bonaparte?"

"It is," I say, and Hawkins stops.

"Ah, for Christ's sake, chum!"

"I mean it, chum," I say.

"You don't sound as if you meant it."

"If he doesn't mean it, I do," says Donovan, working himself up.

"What have you against me, Jeremiah Donovan?"

"I never said I had anything against you. But why did your people take out four of our prisoners and shoot them in cold blood?"

He took Hawkins by the arm and dragged him on, but it was impossible to make him understand that we were in earnest. I had the Smith and Wesson in my pocket and I kept fingering it and wondering what I'd do if they put up a fight for it or ran, and wishing to God they'd do one or the other. I knew if they did run for it, that I'd never fire on them. Hawkins wanted to know was Noble in it, and when we said yes, he asked us why Noble wanted to plug him. Why did any of us want to plug him? What had he done to us? Weren't we all chums? Didn't we understand him and didn't he understand us? Did we imagine for an instant that he'd shoot us for all the so-and-so officers in the so-and-so British Army?

By this time we'd reached the bog, and I was so sick I couldn't even answer him. We walked along the edge of it in the darkness, and every now and then Hawkins would call a halt and begin all over again, as if he was wound up, about our being chums, and I knew that nothing but the sight of the grave would convince him that we had to do it. And all the time I was hoping that something would happen; that they'd run for it or that Noble would take over the responsibility from me. I had the feeling that it was worse on Noble than on me.

IV

At last we saw the lantern in the distance and made towards it. Noble was carrying it, and Feeney was standing somewhere in the darkness behind him, and the picture of them so still and silent in the bogland brought it home to me that we were in earnest, and banished the last bit of hope I had.

Belcher, on recognizing Noble, said: "Hallo, chum," in his quiet way, but Hawkins flew at him at once, and the argument began all over again, only this time Noble had nothing to say for himself and stood with his head down, holding the lantern between his legs.

It was Jeremiah Donovan who did the answering. For the twentieth time, as though it was haunting his mind, Hawkins asked if anybody thought he'd shoot Noble.

"Yes, you would," says Jeremiah Donovan.

"No, I wouldn't, damn you!"

"You would, because you'd know you'd be shot for not doing it."

"I wouldn't, not if I was to be shot twenty times over. I wouldn't shoot a pal. And Belcher wouldn't—isn't that right, Belcher?"

"That's right, chum," Belcher said, but more by way of answering the question than of joining in the argument. Belcher sounded as though whatever unforeseen thing he'd always been waiting for had come at last.

"Anyway, who says Noble would be shot if I wasn't? What do you think I'd do if I was in his place, out in the middle of a blasted bog?"

"What would you do?" asks Donovan.

"I'd go with him wherever he was going, of course. Share my last bob with him and stick by him through thick and thin. No one can ever say of me that I let down a pal."

"We had enough of this," says Jeremiah Donovan, cocking his revolver. "Is there any message you want to send?"

"No, there isn't."

"Do you want to say your prayers?"

Hawkins came out with a cold-blooded remark that even shocked me and turned on Noble again.

"Listen to me, Noble," he says. "You and me are chums. You can't come over to my side, so I'll come over to your side. That show you I mean what I say? Give me a rifle and I'll go along with you and the other lads."

Nobody answered him. We knew that was no way out.

"Hear what I'm saying?" he says. "I'm through with it. I'm a deserter or anything else you like. I don't believe in your stuff, but it's no worse than mine. That satisfy you?"

Noble raised his head, but Donovan began to speak and he lowered it again without replying.

"For the last time, have you any messages to send?" says Donovan in a cold, excited sort of voice.

"Shut up, Donovan! You don't understand me, but these lads do. They're not the sort to make a pal and kill a pal. They're not the tools of any capitalist."

I alone of the crowd saw Donovan raise his Webley to the back of Hawkins's neck, and as he did so I shut my eyes and tried to pray. Hawkins had begun to say something else when Donovan fired, and as I opened my eyes at the bang, I saw Hawkins stagger at the knees and lie out flat at Noble's feet, slowly and as quiet as a kid falling asleep, with the lantern-light on his lean legs and bright farmer's boots. We all stood very still, watching him settle out in the last agony.

Then Belcher took out a handkerchief and began to tie it about his own eyes (in our excitement we'd forgotten to do the same for Hawkins), and, seeing it wasn't big enough, turned and asked for the loan of mine. I gave it to him and he knotted the two together and pointed with his foot at Hawkins.

"He's not quite dead," he says. "Better give him another."

Sure enough, Hawkins's left knee is beginning to rise. I bend down and put my gun to his head; then, recollecting myself, I get up again. Belcher understands what's in my mind.

"Give him his first," he says. "I don't mind. Poor bastard, we don't know what's happening to him now."

I knelt and fired. By this time I didn't seem to know what I was doing. Belcher, who was fumbling a bit awkwardly with the handkerchiefs, came out with a laugh as he heard the shot. It was the first time I heard him laugh and it sent a shudder down my back; it sounded so unnatural.

"Poor bugger!" he said quietly. "And last night he was so curious about it all. It's very queer, chums, I always think. Now he knows as much about it as they'll ever let him know, and last night he was all in the dark."

Donovan helped him to tie the handkerchiefs about his eyes. "Thanks, chum," he said. Donovan asked if there were any messages he wanted sent.

"No, chum," he says. "Not for me. If any of you would like to write to Hawkins's mother, you'll find a letter from her in his pocket. He and his mother were great chums. But my missus left me eight years ago. Went away with another fellow and took the kid with her. I like the feeling of a home, as you may have noticed, but I couldn't start again after that."

It was an extraordinary thing, but in those few minutes Belcher said more than in all the weeks before. It was just as if the sound of the shot had started a flood of talk in him and he could go on the whole night like that, quite happily, talking about himself. We stood round like fools now that he couldn't see us any longer. Donovan looked at Noble, and Noble shook his head. Then Donovan raised his Webley, and at that moment Belcher gives his queer laugh again. He may have thought we were talking about him, or perhaps he noticed the same thing I'd noticed and couldn't understand it.

"Excuse me, chums," he says. "I feel I'm talking the hell of a lot, and so silly, about my being so handy about a house and things like that. But this thing came on me suddenly. You'll forgive me, I'm sure."

"You don't want to say a prayer?" asks Donovan.

"No, chum," he says. "I don't think it would help. I'm ready, and you boys want to get it over."

"You understand that we're only doing our duty?" says Donovan.

Belcher's head was raised like a blind man's, so that you could only see his chin and the tip of his nose in the lantern-light.

"I never could make out what duty was myself," he said. "I think you're all good lads, if that's what you mean. I'm not complaining."

Noble, just as if he couldn't bear any more of it, raised

his fist at Donovan, and in a flash Donovan raised his gun and fired. The big man went over like a sack of meal, and this time there was no need of a second shot.

I don't remember much about the burying, but that it was worse than all the rest because we had to carry them to the grave. It was all mad lonely with nothing but a patch of lantern-light between ourselves and the dark, and birds hooting and screeching all round, disturbed by the guns. Noble went through Hawkins's belongings to find the letter from his mother, and then joined his hands together. He did the same with Belcher. Then, when we'd filled in the grave, we separated from Jeremiah Donovan and Feeney and took our tools back to the shed. All the way we didn't speak a word. The kitchen was dark and cold as we'd left it, and the old woman was sitting over the hearth, saying her beads. We walked past her into the room, and Noble struck a match to light the lamp. She rose quietly and came to the doorway with all her cantankerousness gone.

"What did ye do with them?" she asked in a whisper, and Noble started so that the match went out in his hand.

"What's that?" he asked without turning round.

"I heard ye," she said.

"What did you hear?" asked Noble.

"I heard ye. Do ye think I didn't hear ye, putting the spade back in the houseen?"

Noble struck another match and this time the lamp lit for him.

"Was that what ye did to them?" she asked.

Then, by God, in the very doorway, she fell on her knees and began praying, and after looking at her for a minute or two Noble did the same by the fireplace. I pushed my way out past her and left them at it. I stood at the door, watching the stars and listening to the shrieking of the birds dying out over the bogs. It is so strange what you feel at times like that that you can't describe it. Noble says he saw everything ten times the size, as though there were nothing in the whole world but that little patch of bog with the two Englishmen stiffening into it, but with me it was as if the patch of bog where the Englishmen were was a million miles away, and even Noble and the old woman, mumbling behind me, and the birds and the bloody stars were all far away, and I was

> somehow very small and very lost and lonely like a child astray in the snow. And anything that happened to me afterwards, I never felt the same about again.

CHOOSING THE SUBJECT

As we read and react to "Guests of the Nation," certain ideas are bound to come into our minds, and we will probably ask some questions: How did O'Connor get us so involved in this story? Did Hawkins and Belcher have to die? Why didn't Noble and Bonaparte do something more to prevent the killings? What kinds of people are we reading about? Why is Bonaparte the one who tells the story? Does military duty have to work this way? What is the author saying about duty? Must men always do as they are told? In a course on the short story you might be asked whether the Irish soldiers' duty was to kill the Englishmen.

The answers to such questions can come in part from a consideration of the kinds of questions that we have previously raised about reading short stories. The discussion of point of view throws light on how the writer presented the elements of his story. We tend to identify with Bonaparte who tells the story and our interpretation of its meaning is conditioned by what he knows at various times and how he reacts to the killing.

We see the cause and effect development of the plot—why each event happened as it did. We can consider how much choice Noble and Bonaparte had in their possibilities for action. We can see the reversal of Bonaparte's situation and what he learned in the course of the story.

We will draw inferences about the characters from their actions. We can observe how the focus is kept on Bonaparte and how he is affected by what he goes through. We can consider what each character contributes to the action or to the characterization of Bonaparte.

What the setting contributes to the action will draw some of our attention. Finally, there is the significance of the story, its theme. How has the author interpreted the action to give it meaning?

Any of the major elements of a story (point of view, plot,

character, setting, or theme) are suitable topics for critical papers. As you choose one, consider the earlier discussion and questions on the element that you choose.

1. Frank O'Connor as artist
2. Suspense in "Guests of the Nation"
3. Characterization in "Guests of the Nation"
4. The theme of duty in "Guests of the Nation"

Next consider what can be said about the topics. One way of doing that is to put a topic in the form of questions. In the first possible topic above, you might ask in what ways is O'Connor an artist? Then consider your answer by carrying on a dialogue with yourself. The word *artist* is vague. Does it mean that he writes in a particularly artistic way, as opposed to other writers? What does *artistic* mean? With which other writers can he be compared? Can a writer be judged on the basis of one story? Is the story typical of the way that he writes? It seems clear at this point that too many questions are piling up. The answers would demand a book rather than an essay. The topic is best discarded.

In considering the second possible topic, ask what devices are used to create suspense and maintain it throughout the story? The problem of suspense, of what will happen to Belcher and Hawkins, was settled quickly. Suspense is not a major factor in the story and is best discarded as a topic for a critical essay.

The third suggestion, on characterization, lends itself to the questions, What are the people in the story like? By what methods are they characterized?

The topic suggests that we deal with all the characters. Belcher is a big, good-natured Englishman, willing to help around the house by carrying water or cutting wood, generally agreeing with anyone, and revealing his past only when he is about to die. Hawkins is a contrasting character—short, talkative, always willing to argue religion with Noble, "whose brother was a priest," and Hawkins is willing to fight on any side to save his own life.

Opposed to the Englishmen, we have the Irish. Noble is religious, but not quick enough to argue with Hawkins. Hating the idea of killing, Noble, whose name is part of the characterization, prefers to dig the grave. Jeremiah Donovan is an officer of some kind who takes orders from those who outrank him and hands them on to the younger men, Noble and Bonaparte. Donovan believes in army discipline and has no compunctions about killing. Bonaparte is the central character, and his voice tells the story. It is he who is most affected by having to carry out the duty of killing the hostages whom he has grown to like. It is he who watches the execution, is forced to take part in it, and says at the end, "And anything that happened to me afterwards, I never felt the same about again."

There are two more minor characters. Feeney is "the local intelligence officer," who does little except represent the authority of the larger army within whose concept of duty the men must act. His appearance makes it less likely that the execution can be avoided. Finally there is the old woman who runs the house in which Belcher and Hawkins are being held as hostages and who is befriended by Belcher. It is she who reminds us of the religious motif (a repeated theme) in the story, especially when she kneels and prays at the end, reminding Noble and Bonaparte that there may be more to religion than Hawkins would admit, and that killing violates one of its central principles. Certainly we could write at some length on the characterizations by offering evidence for all these general ideas.

The fourth topic, on the theme of duty, is the most important one for this story. Each of the soldiers has a different sense of duty. For Donovan, everything is clear: if the English kill Irish prisoners, the Irish must shoot the English prisoners in return. For Noble and Bonaparte, the issue is more complex: should they kill their friends? Noble is a religious man; he cannot kill easily and chooses to dig the graves. Bonaparte hopes that the two soldiers will run and get away. When Donovan talks of duty, Bonaparte says to the reader, "I never noticed that people who talk a lot about duty find it much of a trouble to them." Notice the irony of his being named after one of the leading military figures in history.

HOW TO TAKE NOTES FOR THE PAPER

If you now decide to write on the main theme of this story, you will want to consider such questions as these: What concept of duty does each of the characters have? Can a man have more than one duty? To what? Can men's various duties conflict with one another? How does the meaning of duty shift as the story goes on? What attitude is the author taking toward duty? What point is he making in the story?

A writer should always be listening to the voice of an imaginary reader saying: What do you mean by that word or idea? Why do you believe that? As you review the story, you will find answers that convince you. To convince your reader, you will need specific items in the story to support your statements. A good way to make notes of these is to use 3 x 5 cards or pads, putting one note on each slip; in this way you can organize and reorganize your ideas without recopying each time. When you make a note, indicate the page on which you found it. Refer to incidents in such language that the reader could identify the page and the incident being discussed. Sometimes this is done by quoting a single word or phrase: "deserter" or "No one can ever say of me that I let down a pal." Or one can summarize: Donovan shot Hawkins. Do not use vague phrases like, We learn about Hawkins from the way he acted when he was about to be shot. Tell the reader how Hawkins acted; be specific.

When quoting directly, use quotation marks around the exact words taken from the text. (Hawkins argued that he never "let down a pal.") If you omit words within a quotation, mark the omission with an ellipsis, three spaced periods (. . .). ("Noble says he saw everything ten times the size, as though there were nothing in the whole world but that little patch of bog . . . and I was somehow very small and very lost and lonely like a child astray in the snow.") To indicate words omitted at the end of a sentence, use the three periods and add a fourth, the true period that marks the end of the sentence. ("Then, by God, in the very doorway, she fell on her knees and began praying. . . .")*

Remember that when a specific reference is made, a reader should be able to put his finger on the spot of the page that you are discussing. The function of specific references is to give evidence for the truth of the general statements made about the work. If, for example, you say that an eerie atmosphere is created at the time of the execution, the statement needs to be sup-

* For a fuller discussion of how to quote, see Appendix, p. 193.

ported by your saying something about the setting, the darkness and the lighting.

SELECTING THE NOTES

In this paper we are writing on duty, so our notes will be on the major references to that topic:

1. Noble and Bonaparte are assigned to guard Belcher and Hawkins.
2. After the card games and dances, "we gave up all pretence of keeping a close eye on them."
3. Old woman argues that war was started because a "heathen divinity" was stolen. Adds, "nothing but sorrow and want can follow the people that disturb the hidden powers." Foreshadowing.
4. Hawkins argues that love of country is manipulated by capitalists and priests.
5. Noble argues for religion and the "next world."
6. Noble and Bonaparte want to end guard duty and join "a fighting column." Learn that Hawkins and Belcher are hostages.
7. Donovan—"If they shoot our prisoners, we'll shoot theirs."
8. Bonaparte wants to explain about "an old dog going to the vet's," but realizes that Donovan would not understand affection.
9. Donovan announces execution of Irish soldiers and the need for reprisal.
10. Noble wants to be left out; is sent to dig graves.
11. When execution is arranged for, Donovan talks of duty.
12. Bonaparte—"I never noticed that people who talk a lot about duty find it much of a trouble to them."
13. Bonaparte hopes the prisoners will run, knowing "I'd never fire on them."
14. When Hawkins continues to argue that he would never shoot a pal, Donovan says that he would, "because you'd know that you'd be shot for not doing it."
15. Hawkins offers to be a deserter.
16. Bonaparte adds a shot at Hawkins because he seems to be still alive.
17. Belcher—"I could never make out what duty was myself."

18. Old woman "fell on her knees and began praying," pointing up the conflict between religious duty and military duty.
19. Bonaparte—"And anything that happened to me afterwards, I never felt the same about again."

The notes fall into major classifications: what each person sees as his duty, the reaction of each to the execution, and a conflict between military duty and religious duty. Donovan and Hawkins are not moved by religious ideas; Belcher is non-commital, but is kind to others; Noble and Bonaparte are moved by religious impulses. The old woman moves in the background, keeping the religious motif alive ("the hidden powers").

ORGANIZING THE NOTES

The numbered notes represent the references to duty, the topic of our paper, in the order in which the incidents occur in the story. Now we should determine some more logical connections between them. We can see, with a few overlapping exceptions, that each note applies to a particular character in the story. If we reshuffle our notes, we can arrange them according to the character referred to in each, keeping in mind any notes that refer to more than one character.

It is apparent that some characters are more important than others. In what order should we discuss them? It is clear that Bonaparte is the leading character. He appears in every scene, tells the story, reacts to what happens; and we have more material about him than about any of the others. By discussing him last, we lead into the total meaning of the story.

We can, then, arrange a discussion of the characters according to their importance in the meaning of the story. Hawkins and Belcher might come first; they are minor characters who are acted on by others. Donovan can stand alone as a middle figure against whom both sides are revolting. Noble and Bonaparte are those most affected mentally by the execution. Since Bonaparte is the one whose reaction makes the story, we can consider him last. Where, then, should we discuss the old woman? We can put her just before Noble and Bonaparte as a transitional figure; she adds to the religious conflict in the story.

Now we can reorganize our notes by reordering them and by

making brief references to the material on our cards. Then we will have a partial outline of the paper.

Belcher
- Does not understand what duty is

Hawkins
- Love of country is a fraud
- Rejects religious values
- Wouldn't shoot a pal
- Offers to be a deserter

Donovan
- One side kills hostages if the other side does
- Executes captives from feeling of duty
- If duty is not carried out, a man is shot

Old woman
- The "hidden powers" should not be disturbed
- Prays after execution

Noble
- Guard of prisoners, as is Bonaparte
- Cards and dances make friends of guards and prisoners
- Argues religion ("next world") with Hawkins
- Wants to join regular army
- Avoids execution; digs graves

Bonaparte
- Guard, friend
- Contrast to Donovan, in affection for prisoners
- Bothered by Donovan's talk of duty
- Hopes the prisoners will run
- Shoots only to keep Hawkins from suffering
- Greatly moved by the incident

DEVELOPING THE THESIS STATEMENT

Once the topic is selected and notes bearing on the issue are listed and organized, you must decide on what is to be said about the subject. To develop a topic into a thesis, the writer evolves a sentence, the statement of an idea that can be argued by reference to the notes.

It is clear that this story deals with various views of duty. When we look at our notes, we can see that a sense of duty can drive people to certain actions. But once the main action is carried out, we see the effect on the characters. This cause and effect relation should be expressed in the thesis statement. It might then read: In "Guests of the Nation" Frank O'Connor portrays his characters acting out their ideas of duty, and shows how each is affected by carrying out his ideas.

What has been done in making this sentence is to state relationships between the notes made earlier. Also built into the statement is an implied outline of the general ideas to be developed and supported in the essay: ". . . characters . . . ideas of duty . . . how each is affected. . . ." Or to put the ideas in the form of questions to be answered: What does each character in turn consider his duty to be? How is each character affected by his ideas on duty? Then, in order to relate the paper to the main intent of the story, we should consider the question of what O'Connor seems to think man's duty is. If we look carefully at the notes and the story, we see that two kinds of duty seem to dominate—military duty and religious duty.

STARTING THE ESSAY

It is customary to begin essays in one of the following ways:

Topic Statement

In "Guests of the Nation," Frank O'Connor dramatizes the idea that men have more than one duty, even in time of war.

Quotation

In writing about short stories, Frank O'Connor said, "Generations of skillful stylists from Chekhov to Katherine Mansfield and James Joyce had so fashioned the short story that it no longer rang with the tone of a man's voice, speaking."

Direct Statement

A person can do his duty and yet do wrong according to his conscience.

Analogy

Any man who obeys orders and who does his duty by carrying out acts repugnant to him becomes like Hitler's generals, who justified their acts by saying that they must carry out orders.

Personal Definition

Duty is what one owes to his conscience or to God, to his country, to an organization, or to another person. Clearly a man can have more than one duty.

Suspenseful Question

Forced into a situation in which he is asked to kill a friend, what should a man do?

OPENINGS TO BE AVOIDED

Don't begin with a dictionary definition ("According to Webster, duty is conduct owed to older people"). The meaning chosen from the dictionary may not fit the meaning of the story and, if it does, will be dull. Don't begin with specific details from the story ("Belcher and Hawkins are British soldiers who have been captured by the Irish army"). Before you supply details, you need to let the reader know what you are talking about.

Don't tell who the author is and where he was born; that information is not within the topic to be discussed.

Don't refer to the title of your paper ("This topic is . . ."). The title is a message to the reader; it is not part of the paper.

Don't use a personal point of view ("I think . . . , and you will see . . ."). The reader will know what the writer thinks without being told.

CHOOSING A TITLE

An arresting title will help the reader to focus on what you are writing about: Conflicts in Duty, The Duties of Men, The Duty to Choose, A Challenge to War, Duty or Friendship, or any other that you prefer.

DEVELOPING THE THESIS

Here the word *thesis* means the main idea that you intend to discuss. When you write your paper, you state your thesis in a general statement to guide your reader.

However the paper begins, the main ideas should be stated in general terms near the beginning; the specific evidence will be presented in the body of the paper. In the development of the thesis, the main ideas will form the outline, the order of the discussion. They will also suggest a structure for the paragraphs:

character, idea of duty, and consequences. The meaning of each general statement and its key words must be clear. Each paragraph should be developed by offering specific evidence for the truth of the statement.

ENDING THE ESSAY

An ending may consider the relationship of what you have said to the theme of the story or may comment on the main idea in a different way. Do not summarize by merely repeating what you have already said. An ending may also suggest an analogy by referring to a similar situation known to the writer. If a person objects to a war, for example, should he allow himself to be drafted?

REVISING THE FIRST DRAFT

After making a draft of your essay, reread it carefully. Is each paragraph after the general statements made up of a general statement and the evidence to support it? Is each idea clear and does it lead logically into the next? If the individual sentences were written on separate cards and shuffled, could the original order be reconstructed by a reader? Is everything said as simply as possible? Can any unnecessary words or phrases be crossed out? Are the pronoun references clear? Does the word *and* connect words or phrases that logically and grammatically go together? Are there any unnecessary repetitions of ideas? If words or phrases are quoted directly from the story, are quotation marks used?

Are the tenses consistent? If the paper says, "Belcher and Hawkins *are* British soldiers," the verbs should continue to describe the action in the present tense and not shift to "Donovan *shot* the two men." A writer can discuss a story as though it is happening in the present (Donovan says that the men must be executed.) or as though it happened in the past (Donovan said that it was his duty.), but he must be consistent. However, if a statement in the paper is made on a historical point (The story was published in 1931.), the writer must describe it as having happened in the past.

If the action being described happened before the story began, if it is part of the exposition, the writer can describe it with a past tense (Belcher and Hawkins had been transferred to the house to keep the British from finding them.).

Consider that the story itself still lives in the imagination of the writer, and it lives as a person reads it. For that reason it is usually better to write as though the story were happening as you write your paper.

A formal paper requires formal diction: do not fall into colloquial expressions or slang.

The relations between ideas, sentences, or paragraphs can be clarified, when necessary, by transitions, such as the following:

- for additional ideas: and, furthermore, in addition, moreover, likewise, also, too
- for contrasts: but, in spite of, yet, however, on the contrary, in contrast, on the other hand
- to express results: so, therefore, thus, accordingly, as a result, in consequence, consequently

Other forms of transitions are pronouns, synonyms, or restatements of an idea in different words.

The writer assumes that the reader knows the work that is being discussed, but he must show his understanding of it by pointing out relationships between the parts of the story.

In typing a paper (double spaced for easy reading), leave inch-and-a-half margins at the top, bottom, and sides. Proofread the paper before handing it in. To cut a word or phrase, draw a horizontal line through the words to be cut. To insert words, put a caret (‸) under the appropriate space and write clearly above the line what you want to add.

The following is an example of what your final essay should be like.

The Duties of Men

In "Guests of the Nation," Frank O'Connor dramatizes the idea that men have more than one kind of duty, even in time of war. He portrays his characters acting out their different ideas of duty, what it means to each of them, and how each is affected by his own actions. Those characters who understand the complexity of the problem are deeply moved by being involved in an execution in the name of military duty.

The complication in the plot is whether Belcher and Hawkins, British soldiers being held as hostages, should be killed by the Irish guards who have become their friends. But the order comes; the Englishmen must die.

Belcher is big, good-natured, and willing to agree with anyone. "That's right, chum," is his usual contribution to the conversation. He endears himself to the old woman in whose house they are being kept by chopping her wood and carrying her loads. His guards, Noble and Bonaparte, like him because he plays cards and attends dances with them. When he knows that he must die, he forgives his executors, "I think you're all good lads. . . ." When confronted by Donovan's talk of duty, he says, "I never could make out what duty was myself." The friendly feelings of Noble and Bonaparte toward Belcher are reinforced when he reveals something of his past, ". . . my missus left me eight years ago. Went away with another fellow and took the kid with her. I like the feeling of a home, as you may have noticed. . . ." He accepts suffering without complaint: it is now his duty to die; although he does not understand why, he does not question it.

Hawkins, in the same position as Belcher, has no sense of military duty. He is a contrast to Belcher in being small, argumentative, cynical, and self-serving. He dismisses duty to country as a plot of capitalists, ". . . the first thing your God created was a bleeding capitalist, with morality and Rolls-Royce complete." He argues with Noble that religion is a fraud. Hawkins "never did a stroke of work," and when he is about to die, argues that he would never "kill a pal." Then he offers to join the Irish army as a deserter from the British army. Hawkins supports the argument that there is no duty beyond that of friendship.

Donovan is a minor officer in the Irish army who accepts only the idea of military duty. If the English kill prisoners, then the Irish must do the same. Donovan is not moved by friendship; Bonaparte says, ". . . it suddenly struck me that he had no great love for the two Englishmen." When Hawkins claims that he would not shoot the Irish guard Noble, Donovan argues, "You would, because you'd know you'd be shot for not doing it," revealing something of his own motivation. Donovan represents the code of the military. He shoots both Hawkins and Belcher.

The old woman in whose house Belcher and Hawkins are being guarded serves as a constant reminder of religious values. Belcher helps in her chores, and Hawkins tries to argue religion with her. She is not very rational, but she does make the statement that "nothing but sorrow and want can follow the people that disturb the hidden powers." The phrase suggests that men have no right to try to go against the will of the supernatural and serves as the central theme of the story. After Belcher and Hawkins are shot, she falls on her knees and prays, presumably for them; perhaps, too, for those who took part in the execution.

Noble, whose name suggests his character, is paired with Bonaparte as being opposed to the execution. As a guard to the prisoners, he, like Bonaparte, plays cards and goes to dances with them. Consequently, he grows to like the men, even though Hawkins continually argues against Noble's deep-seated religious beliefs. Though Noble is not quick enough to defend himself against Hawkins's arguments, he is not moved from his own religious position. When the time comes to kill his friends, Noble asks to be excused and is sent to dig the graves. After the burial, he is very depressed by what has happened.

Bonaparte is the leading character in the story; it is he who tells the story. He is present at all times, and we learn how he is driven to take part in an act that is repulsive to him. Bonaparte is a contrast to Donovan in that, like Noble, he bears a real affection for the English prisoners. It is he who learns from Donovan that the Englishmen are hostages, but he does not tell the prisoners. When he hears Donovan coming, he heads him off outside, hoping that the execution will not take place. The presence of Feeney, who represents the power of higher officers, makes the act inevitable.

So Bonaparte is forced by military duty to take part in an act that is repulsive to him. He, unlike Donovan, feels the bond of friendship. When Donovan talks of military duty, Bonaparte observes, "I never noticed that people who talk a lot about duty find it much of a trouble to them." He hopes that the prisoners will run away as they are being taken from the house into the dark bog. He knows that he cannot act against them. After Donovan shoots Hawkins, Bonaparte, at Belcher's request, shoots Hawkins again because he still seems to be alive. Bonaparte's retelling of Belcher's last revelation before he dies, about his wife and child, indicates that he is moved by the story. Back in the house, he sees the old woman and Noble kneel and pray and says, "And anything that happened to me afterwards, I never felt the same about again."

In presenting his story through the consciousness of Bonaparte, Frank O'Connor is portraying the conflict that can be felt by a sensitive man forced by military duty to do something that conflicts with his conscience. Bonaparte is not the killer that is suggested by the historical associations of his name. He is moved by friendship and is affected by the religious feelings of the old woman and of Noble.

His final statement echoes the old woman's statement that "sorrow" will follow those who disturb the "hidden powers." O'Connor is clearly on the side of those who are not bound by one duty. The very word *guests* in the title recalls many historical associations with the sacred duty a host bears toward a guest.

WRITING A CHARACTERIZATION

A common writing assignment is the characterization of a person in a story—what is the leading character like? Ordinarily, the analysis should be related to the theme of the story. Reread the earlier comments on characterization (p. 21) and the questions that follow those comments. Then read the following story.

A CUP OF TEA — Katherine Mansfield

Rosemary Fell was not exactly beautiful. No, you couldn't have called her beautiful. Pretty? Well, if you took her to pieces. . . . But why be so cruel as to take any one to pieces? She was young, brilliant, extremely modern, exquisitely well dressed, amazingly well read in the newest of the new books, and her parties were the most delicious mixture of the really important people and . . . artists—quaint creatures, discoveries of hers, some of them too terrifying for words, but others quite presentable and amusing.

Rosemary had been married two years. She had a duck of a boy. No, not Peter—Michael. And her husband absolutely adored her. They were rich, really rich, not just comfortably well off, which is odious and stuffy and sounds like one's grandparents. But if Rosemary wanted to shop she would go to Paris as you and I would go to Bond Street. If she wanted to buy flowers, the car pulled up at that perfect shop in Regent Street, and Rosemary inside the shop just gazed in her dazzled, rather exotic way, and said: "I want those and those and those. Give me four bunches of those. And that jar of roses. Yes, I'll have all the roses in the jar. No, no lilac. I hate lilac. It's got no shape." The attendant bowed and put the lilac out of sight, as though this was only too true; lilac was dreadfully shapeless. "Give me those stumpy little tulips. Those red and white ones." And she was followed to the car by a thin shopgirl staggering under an immense white paper armful that looked like a baby in long clothes....

One winter afternoon she had been buying something in a little antique shop in Curzon Street. It was a shop she liked. For one thing, one usually had it to oneself. And then the man who kept it was ridiculously fond of serving her. He beamed whenever she came in. He clasped his hands; he was so gratified that he could scarcely speak. Flattery, of course. All the same, there was something...

"You see, madam," he would explain in his low respectful tones, "I love my things. I would rather not part with them than sell them to some one who does not appreciate them, who has not that fine feeling which is so rare...." And, breathing deeply, he unrolled a tiny square of blue velvet and pressed it on the glass counter with his pale finger-tips.

Today it was a little box. He had been keeping it for her. He had shown it to nobody as yet. An exquisite little enamel box with a glaze so fine it looked as though it had been baked in cream. On the lid a minute creature stood under a flowery tree, and a more minute creature still had her arms around his neck. Her hat, really no bigger than a geranium petal, hung from a branch; it had green ribbons. And there was a pink cloud like a watchful cherub floating above their heads. Rosemary took her hands out of her long gloves. She always took off her gloves to examine such things. Yes, she liked it very much. She loved it; it was a great duck. She must have it. And, turning the creamy box, opening and shutting it, she couldn't help noticing how charming her hands were against the blue velvet. The shopman, in some dim cavern of his mind, may have dared to think so too. For he took a pencil, leant over the counter, and his pale bloodless fingers crept timidly towards those rosy, flashing ones, as he murmured gently: "If I may venture to point out to madam, the flowers on the little lady's bodice."

"Charming!" Rosemary admired the flowers. But what

was the price? For a moment the shopman did not seem to hear. Then a murmur reached her. "Twenty-eight guineas, madam."

"Twenty-eight guineas." Rosemary gave no sign. She laid the little box down; she buttoned her gloves again. Twenty-eight guineas. Even if one is rich. . . . She looked vague. She stared at a plump tea-kettle like a plump hen above the shopman's head, and her voice was dreamy as she answered: "Well, keep it for me—will you? I'll . . ."

But the shopman had already bowed as though keeping it for her was all any human being could ask. He would be willing, of course, to keep it for her for ever.

The discreet door shut with a click. She was outside on the step, gazing at the winter afternoon. Rain was falling, and with the rain it seemed the dark came too, spinning down like ashes. There was a cold bitter taste in the air, and the new-lighted lamps looked sad. Sad were the lights in the houses opposite. Dimly they burned as if regretting something. And people hurried by, hidden under their hateful umbrellas. Rosemary felt a strange pang. She pressed her muff to her breast; she wished she had the little box, too, to cling to. Of course, the car was there. She'd only to cross the pavement. But still she waited. There are moments, horrible moments in life, when one emerges from shelter and looks out, and it's awful. One oughtn't to give way to them. One ought to go home and have an extra-special tea. But at the very instant of thinking that, a young girl, thin, dark, shadowy—where had she come from?—was standing at Rosemary's elbow and a voice like a sigh, almost like a sob, breathed: "Madam, may I speak to you a moment?"

"Speak to me?" Rosemary turned. She saw a little battered creature with enormous eyes, some one quite young, no older than herself, who clutched at her coat-collar with reddened hands, and shivered as though she had just come out of the water.

"M-madam," stammered the voice. "Would you let me have the price of a cup of tea?"

"A cup of tea?" There was something simple, sincere in that voice; it wasn't in the least the voice of a beggar. "Then have you no money at all?" asked Rosemary.

"None, madam," came the answer.

"How extraordinary!" Rosemary peered through the dusk, and the girl gazed back at her. How more than extraordinary! And suddenly it seemed to Rosemary such an adventure. It was like something out of a novel by Dostoevsky, this meeting in the dusk. Supposing she took the girl home? Supposing she did do one of those things she was always reading about or seeing on the stage, what would happen? It would be thrilling. And she heard herself saying afterwards to the amazement of her friends: "I simply took her home with me," as she stepped forward and said to that dim person beside her: "Come home to tea with me."

The girl drew back startled. She even stopped shivering for a moment. Rosemary put out a hand and touched her arm. "I mean it," she said, smiling. And she felt how simple and kind her smile was. "Why won't you? Do. Come home with me now in my car and have tea."

"You—you don't mean it, madam," said the girl, and there was pain in her voice.

"But I do," cried Rosemary. "I want you to. To please me. Come along."

The girl put her fingers to her lips and her eyes devoured Rosemary. "You're—you're not taking me to the police station?" she stammered.

"The police station!" Rosemary laughed out. "Why should I be so cruel? No, I only want to make you warm and to hear—anything you care to tell me."

Hungry people are easily led. The footman held the door of the car open, and a moment later they were skimming through the dusk.

"There!" said Rosemary. She had a feeling of triumph as she slipped her hand through the velvet strap. She could have said, "Now I've got you," as she gazed at the little captive she had netted. But of course she meant it kindly. Oh, more than kindly. She was going to prove to this girl that—wonderful things did happen in life, that—fairy godmothers were real, that—rich people had hearts, and that women *were* sisters. She turned impulsively, saying: "Don't be frightened. After all, why shouldn't you come back with me? We're both women. If I'm the more fortunate, you ought to expect . . ."

But happily at that moment, for she didn't know how the sentence was going to end, the car stopped. The bell was rung, the door opened, and with a charming, protecting, almost embracing movement, Rosemary drew the other into the hall. Warmth, softness, light, a sweet scent, all those things so familiar to her she never even thought about them, she watched that other receive. It was fascinating. She was like the little rich girl in her nursery with all the cupboards to open, all the boxes to unpack.

"Come, come upstairs," said Rosemary, longing to begin to be generous. "Come up to my room." And, besides, she wanted to spare this poor little thing from being stared at by the servants; she decided as they mounted the stairs she would not even ring for Jeanne, but take off her things by herself. The great thing was to be natural!

And "There!" cried Rosemary again, as they reached her beautiful big bedroom with the curtains drawn, the fire leaping on her wonderful lacquer furniture, her gold cushions and the primrose and blue rugs.

The girl stood just inside the door; she seemed dazed. But Rosemary didn't mind that.

"Come and sit down," she cried, dragging her big chair up to the fire, "in this comfy chair. Come and get warm. You look so dreadfully cold."

"I daren't, madam," said the girl, and she edged backwards.

"Oh, please,"—Rosemary ran forward—"you mustn't be frightened, you mustn't, really. Sit down, and when I've taken off my things we shall go into the next room and have tea and be cozy. Why are you afraid?" And gently she half pushed the thin figure into its deep cradle.

But there was no answer. The girl stayed just as she had been put, with her hands by her sides and her mouth slightly open. To be quite sincere, she looked rather stupid. But Rosemary wouldn't acknowledge it. She leant over her, saying: "Won't you take off your hat? Your pretty hair is all wet. And one is so much more comfortable without a hat, isn't one?"

There was a whisper that sounded like, "Very good, madam," and the crushed hat was taken off.

"Let me help you off with your coat, too," said Rosemary.

The girl stood up. But she held on to the chair with one hand and let Rosemary pull. It was quite an effort. The other scarcely helped her at all. She seemed to stagger like a child, and the thought came and went through Rosemary's mind, that if people wanted helping they must respond a little, just a little, otherwise it became very difficult indeed. And what was she to do with the coat now? She left it on the floor, and the hat too. She was just going to take a cigarette off the mantelpiece when the girl said quickly, but so lightly and strangely: "I'm very sorry, madam, but I'm going to faint. I shall go off, madam, if I don't have something."

"Good heavens, how thoughtless I am!" Rosemary rushed to the bell.

"Tea! Tea at once! And some brandy immediately!"

The maid was gone again, but the girl almost cried out: "No, I don't want no brandy. I never drink brandy. It's a cup of tea I want, madam." And she burst into tears.

It was a terrible and fascinating moment. Rosemary knelt beside her chair.

"Don't cry, poor little thing," she said. "Don't cry." And she gave the other her lace handkerchief. She really was touched beyond words. She put her arm round those thin, birdlike shoulders.

Now at last the other forgot to be shy, forgot everything except that they were both women, and gasped out: "I can't go on no longer like this. I can't bear it. I shall do away with myself. I can't bear no more."

"You shan't have to. I'll look after you. Don't cry any more. Don't you see what a good thing it was that you met me? We'll have tea and you'll tell me everything. And I shall arrange something. I promise. *Do* stop crying. It's so exhausting. Please!"

The other did stop just in time for Rosemary to get up before the tea came. She had the table placed between them. She plied the poor little creature with everything, all the sandwiches, all the bread and butter, and every time her cup was empty she filled it with tea, cream and sugar. People always said sugar was so nourishing. As for herself she didn't eat; she smoked and looked away tactfully so that the other should not be shy.

And really the effect of that slight meal was marvelous. When the tea-table was carried away a new being, a light, frail creature with tangled hair, dark lips, deep, lighted eyes, lay back in the big chair in a kind of sweet languor looking at the blaze. Rosemary lit a fresh cigarette; it was time to begin.

"And when did you have your last meal?" she asked softly.

But at that moment the door-handle turned.

"Rosemary, may I come in?" It was Philip.

"Of course."

He came in. "Oh, I'm so sorry," he said, and stopped and stared.

"It's quite all right," said Rosemary, smiling. "This is my friend, Miss—"

"Smith, madam," said the languid figure, who was strangely still and unafraid.

"Smith," said Rosemary. "We are going to have a little talk."

"Oh, yes," said Philip. "Quite," and his eye caught sight of the coat and hat on the floor. He came over to the fire and turned his back to it. "It's a beastly afternoon," he said curiously, still looking at that listless figure, looking at its hands and boots, and then at Rosemary again.

"Yes, isn't it?" said Rosemary enthusiastically. "Vile."

Philip smiled his charming smile. "As a matter of fact," said he, "I wanted you to come into the library for a moment. Would you? Will Miss Smith excuse us?"

The big eyes were raised to him, but Rosemary answered for her. "Of course she will." And they went out of the room together.

"I say," said Philip, when they were alone. "Explain. Who is she? What does it all mean?"

Rosemary, laughing, leaned against the door and said: "I picked her up in Curzon Street. Really. She's a real pick-up. She asked me for the price of a cup of tea, and I brought her home with me."

"But what on earth are you going to do with her?" cried Philip.

"Be nice to her," said Rosemary quickly. "Be frightfully nice to her. Look after her. I don't know how. We haven't talked yet. But show her—treat her—make her feel—"

"My darling girl," said Philip, "you're quite mad, you know. It simply can't be done."

"I knew you'd say that," retorted Rosemary. "Why not? I want to. Isn't that a reason? And besides, one's always reading about these things. I decided—"

"But," said Philip slowly, and he cut the end of a cigar, "she's so astonishingly pretty."

"Pretty?" Rosemary was so surprised that she blushed. "Do you think so? I—I hadn't thought about it."

"Good Lord!" Philip struck a match. "She's absolutely lovely. Look again, my child. I was bowled over when I came into your room just now. However . . . I think you're making a ghastly mistake. Sorry, darling, if I'm crude and all that. But let me know if Miss Smith is going to dine with us in time for me to look up *The Milliner's Gazette.*"

"You absurd creature!" said Rosemary, and she went out of the library, but not back to her bedroom. She went to her writing-room and sat down at her desk. Pretty! Absolutely lovely! Bowled over! Her heart beat like a heavy bell. Pretty! Lovely! She drew her check book towards her. But no, checks would be of no use, of course. She opened a drawer and took out five pound notes, looked at them, put two back, and holding the three squeezed in her hand, she went back to her bedroom.

Half an hour later Philip was still in the library, when Rosemary came in.

"I only wanted to tell you," said she, and she leaned against the door again and looked at him with her dazzled exotic gaze, "Miss Smith won't dine with us tonight."

Philip put down the paper. "Oh, what's happened? Previous engagement?"

Rosemary came over and sat down on his knee. "She insisted on going," said she, "so I gave the poor little thing a present of money. I couldn't keep her against her will, could I?" she added softly.

Rosemary had just done her hair, darkened her eyes a little, and put on her pearls. She put up her hands and touched Philip's cheeks.

"Do you like me?" said she, and her tone, sweet, husky, troubled him.

"I like you awfully," he said, and he held her tighter. "Kiss me."

There was a pause.

Then Rosemary said dreamily, "I saw a fascinating little box today. It cost twenty-eight guineas. May I have it?"

Philip jumped her on his knee. "You may, little wasteful one," said he.

But that was not really what Rosemary wanted to say.

"Philip," she whispered, and she pressed his head against her bosom, "am I *pretty?*"

Katherine Mansfield's method of characterizing Rosemary Fell is subtle. She begins by talking about Rosemary, but she shifts her point of view by occasionally putting into the exposition words that Rosemary would use, without supplying quotation marks. Beginning with the sixth sentence ("She was young, brilliant, extremely modern, . . ."), Katherine Mansfield uses a string of clichés, to represent the way Rosemary thinks.

The Mansfield method of dropping into Rosemary's way of talking continues in the second paragraph in words and phrases like "duck"; "absolutely adored her"; "perfect shop"; "her dazzled, rather exotic way"; "dreadfully shapeless." Watch for other examples. When Rosemary says, "I hate lilac. It's got no shape," the attendant puts the lilac "out of sight." But it is the voice of the writer that adds, "as though this was only too true." The mixing of Rosemary's voice with that of the writer results in a delicate irony.

The problem of making a characterization is, as we said earlier, the matching of a character's thoughts, speeches, and actions with the reader's conclusion about what they mean. In the lilac example, we might infer that since lilacs are cheaper than roses, Rosemary is extravagant; we are helped to make this inference by the context. The meaning is supplied by the reader in the form of a descriptive word, *extravagant*. When a reader adds up the various descriptive phrases, he has his characterization. Even in this brief story, we learn a good deal about Rosemary.

She is pretty, or is she? We are left with some doubts in the opening lines and again at the end, but the idea is important to Rosemary. She is accustomed to luxury and is self-indulgent. She loves admiration. Her desire for things seems to be an armor against loneliness; yet things are more important to her than people, who are used by her. The major action of the story, her bringing home the girl for a cup of tea, brings Rosemary's insecurities to a head when her husband says, "But she's so astonishingly pretty." Rosemary is selfish in dealing with her guest, lies to her husband about why the girl leaves, and makes a final bid for attention that brings to focus all of her self-doubts.

These general statements are a summary of the main characteristics that are revealed in the story. To write a paper, we should match them with evidence. To that end we can sketch an outline.

MAKING NOTES FOR THE PAPER

1. Pretty?
   "not exactly beautiful"
   Contrast husband's remark "But she's so astonishingly pretty" with "Philip, am I *pretty?*"
2. Accustomed to luxury
   Used to shopping in Paris and "perfect" shops
   Extravagance in buying flowers
   Wants the "little enamel box" (which ironically portrays lovers)
3. Fond of admiration
   Man in store "beamed whenever she came in"
   She admires her hands "against the blue velvet"
   At end she fixes herself up and asks, "Philip, am I *pretty?*"
4. Lonely
   Setting as she leaves the store is a comment on her life: sad mood is suggested by words and images: *rain, dark, sad,* shut off from people by umbrellas
   "There are moments, horrible moments in life, when one emerges from shelter and looks out, and it's awful." (Theme of story)
5. People are to be used
   Motive for taking girl home is to make an impression on her friends
   Irony of "She was going to prove . . . that women were sisters."
   Husband's admiration makes Rosemary decide to send girl away.
6. People are less important than things
   Contrast "took out five pound notes, . . . put two back," with "I saw a fascinating little box today. It cost twenty-eight guineas. May I have it?"

DEVELOPING THE THESIS STATEMENT

On the basis of the story and our notes, we can now make a summarizing statement that can serve as a thesis statement for a paper on the character of Rosemary Fell.

Katherine Mansfield's "A Cup of Tea" is a portrait of Rosemary Fell, a self-centered, materialistic woman, grasping for admiration, whose failure to communicate with other people makes her doubt even her relationship with her husband.

EXERCISE

Using the above notes and the thesis statement, write a characterization of Rosemary Fell. Remember that your problem is to show what she is like. Also, relate the characterization to the total meaning of the story. How does Rosemary emerge "from shelter" in this story? Why is it "horrible"? What does she learn? You may of course use any ideas in the story that are not in the notes.

COUNTERPARTS

James Joyce

The bell rang furiously and, when Miss Parker went to the tube, a furious voice called out in a piercing North of Ireland accent:

"Send Farrington here!"

Miss Parker returned to her machine, saying to a man who was writing at a desk:

"Mr. Alleyne wants you upstairs."

The man muttered *"Blast* him!" under his breath and pushed back his chair to stand up. When he stood up he was tall and of great bulk. He had a hanging face, dark wine-coloured, with fair eyebrows and moustache: his eyes bulged forward slightly and the whites of them were dirty. He lifted up the counter and, passing by the clients, went out of the office with a heavy step.

He went heavily upstairs until he came to the second landing, where a door bore a brass plate with the inscription *Mr. Alleyne.* Here he halted, puffing with labour and vexation, and knocked. The shrill voice cried:

"Come in!"

The man entered Mr. Alleyne's room. Simultaneously Mr. Alleyne, a little man wearing gold-rimmed glasses on a clean-shaven face, shot his head up over a pile of documents. The head itself was so pink and hairless it seemed like a large egg reposing on the papers. Mr. Alleyne did not lose a moment:

"Farrington? What is the meaning of this? Why have I always to complain of you? May I ask you why you haven't made a copy of that contract between Bodley and Kirwan? I told you it must be ready by four o'clock."

"But Mr. Shelley said, sir—"

"Mr. Shelley said, sir.... Kindly attend to what I say and not to what *Mr. Shelley says, sir.* You have always some excuse or another for shirking work. Let me tell you that if the contract is not copied before this evening I'll lay the matter before Mr. Crosbie.... Do you hear me now?"

"Yes, sir."

"Do you hear me now?... Ay and another little matter! I might as well be talking to the wall as talking to you. Understand once for all that you get a half an hour for your lunch and not an hour and a half. How many courses do you want, I'd like to know.... Do you mind me now?"

"Yes, sir."

Mr. Alleyne bent his head again upon his pile of papers. The man stared fixedly at the polished skull which directed the affairs of Crosbie & Alleyne, gauging its fragility. A spasm of rage gripped his throat for a few moments and then passed, leaving after it a sharp sensation of thirst. The man recognized the sensation and felt that he must have a good night's drinking. The middle of the month was passed and, if he could get the copy done in time, Mr. Alleyne might give him an order on the cashier. He stood still, gazing fixedly at the head upon the pile of papers. Suddenly Mr. Alleyne began to upset all the papers, searching for something. Then, as if he had been unaware of the man's presence till that moment, he shot up his head again, saying:

"Eh? Are you going to stand there all day? Upon my word, Farrington, you take things easy!"

"I was waiting to see..."

"Very good, you needn't wait to see. Go downstairs and do your work."

The man walked heavily towards the door and, as he went out of the room, he heard Mr. Alleyne cry after him that if the contract was not copied by evening Mr. Crosbie would hear of the matter.

He returned to his desk in the lower office and counted the sheets which remained to be copied. He took up his pen and dipped it in the ink but he continued to stare stupidly at the last words he had written: *In no case shall the said Bernard Bodley be...* The evening was falling and in a few minutes they would be lighting the gas: then he could write. He felt that he must slake the thirst in his throat. He stood up from his desk and, lifting the counter as before, passed out of the office. As he was passing out the chief clerk looked at him inquiringly.

"It's all right, Mr. Shelley," said the man, pointing his finger to indicate the objective of his journey.

The chief clerk glanced at the hat-rack, but, seeing the row complete, offered no remark. As soon as he was on the landing the man pulled a shepherd's plaid cap out of his pocket, put it on his head and ran quickly down the rickety stairs. From the street door he walked on furtively on the inner side of the path towards the corner and all at once dived into a doorway. He was now safe in the dark snug of O'Neill's shop, and filling up the little window that looked into the bar with his inflamed face, the colour of dark wine or dark meat, he called out:

"Here, Pat, give us a g.p., like a good fellow."

The curate brought him a glass of plain porter. The man drank it at a gulp and asked for a caraway seed. He put his penny on the counter and, leaving the curate to grope for it in the gloom, retreated out of the snug as furtively as he had entered it.

Darkness, accompanied by a thick fog, was gaining upon the dusk of February and the lamps in Eustace Street had been lit. The man went up by the houses until he reached the door of the office, wondering whether he could finish his copy in time. On the stairs a moist pungent odour of perfumes saluted his nose: evidently Miss Delacour had come while he was out in O'Neill's. He crammed his cap back again into his pocket and re-entered the office, assuming an air of absentmindedness.

"Mr. Alleyne has been calling for you," said the chief clerk severely. "Where were you?"

The man glanced at the two clients who were standing at the counter as if to intimate that their presence prevented him from answering. As the clients were both male the chief clerk allowed himself a laugh.

"I know that game," he said. "Five times in one day is a little bit... Well, you better look sharp and get a copy of our correspondence in the Delacour case for Mr. Alleyne."

This address in the presence of the public, his run upstairs and the porter he had gulped down so hastily confused the man and, as he sat down at his desk to get what was required, he realised how hopeless was the task of finishing his copy of the contract before half past five. The dark damp night was coming and he longed to spend it in the bars, drinking with his friends amid the glare of gas and the clatter of glasses. He got out the Delacour correspondence and passed out of the office. He hoped Mr. Alleyne would not discover that the last two letters were missing.

The moist pungent perfume lay all the way up to Mr. Alleyne's room. Miss Delacour was a middle-aged woman of Jewish appearance. Mr. Alleyne was said to be sweet on her or on her money. She came to the office often and stayed a long time when she came. She was sitting beside his desk now in an aroma of perfumes, smoothing the handle of her umbrella and nodding the great black feather in her hat. Mr. Alleyne had swivelled his chair round to face her and thrown his right foot jauntily upon his left knee. The man put the correspondence on the desk and bowed respectfully but neither Mr. Alleyne nor Miss Delacour took any notice of his bow. Mr. Alleyne tapped a finger on the correspondence and then flicked it towards him as if to say: *"That's all right: you can go."*

The man returned to the lower office and sat down again at his desk. He stared intently at the incomplete phrase: *In no case shall the said Bernard Bodley be . . .* and thought how strange it was that the last three words began with the same letter. The chief clerk began to hurry Miss Parker, saying she would never have the letters typed in time for post. The man listened to the clicking of the machine for a few minutes and then set to work to finish his copy. But his head was not clear and his mind wandered away to the glare and rattle of the public-house. It was a night for hot punches. He struggled on with his copy, but when the clock struck five he had still fourteen pages to write. Blast it! He couldn't finish it in time. He longed to execrate aloud, to bring his fist down on something violently. He was so enraged that he wrote *Bernard Bernard* instead of *Bernard Bodley* and had to begin again on a clean sheet.

He felt strong enough to clear out the whole office singlehanded. His body ached to do something, to rush out and revel in violence. All the indignities of his life enraged him. . . . Could he ask the cashier privately for an advance? No, the cashier was no good, no damn good; he wouldn't give an advance.... He knew where he would meet the boys: Leonard and O'Halloran and Nosey Flynn. The barometer of his emotional nature was set for a spell of riot.

His imagination had so abstracted him that his name was called twice before he answered. Mr. Alleyne and Miss Delacour were standing outside the counter and all the clerks had turned round in anticipation of something. The man got up from his desk. Mr. Alleyne began a tirade of abuse, saying that two letters were missing. The man answered that he knew nothing about them, that he had made a faithful copy. The tirade continued: it was so bitter and violent that the man could hardly restrain his fist from descending upon the head of the manikin before him:

"I know nothing about any other two letters," he said stupidly.

"You—know—nothing. Of course you know nothing," said Mr. Alleyne. "Tell me," he added, glancing first for approval to the lady beside him, "do you take me for a fool? Do you think me an utter fool?"

The man glanced from the lady's face to the little egg-shaped head and back again; and, almost before he was aware of it, his tongue had found a felicitous moment:

"I don't think, sir," he said, "that that's a fair question to put to me."

There was a pause in the very breathing of the clerks. Everyone was astounded (the author of the witticism no less than his neighbours) and Miss Delacour, who was a stout amiable person, began to smile broadly. Mr. Alleyne flushed to the hue of a wild rose and his mouth twitched with a dwarf's passion. He shook his fist in the man's face till it seemed to vibrate like the knob of some electric machine:

"You impertinent ruffian! You impertinent ruffian! I'll make short work of you! Wait till you see! You'll apologise to me for your impertinence or you'll quit the office instanter! You'll quit this, I'm telling you, or you'll apologise to me!"

He stood in a doorway opposite the office watching to see if the cashier would come out alone. All the clerks passed out and finally the cashier came out with the chief clerk. It was no use trying to say a word to him when he was with the chief clerk. The man felt that his position was bad enough. He had been obliged to offer an abject apology to Mr. Alleyne for his impertinence but he knew what a hornet's nest the office would be for him. He could remember the way in which Mr. Alleyne had hounded little Peake out of the office in order to make room for his own nephew. He felt savage and thirsty and revengeful, annoyed with himself and with everyone else. Mr. Alleyne would never give him an hour's rest; his life would be a hell to him. He had made a proper fool of himself this time. Could he not keep his tongue in his cheek? But they had never pulled together from the first, he and Mr. Alleyne, ever since the day Mr. Alleyne had overheard him mimicking his North of Ireland accent to amuse Higgins and Miss Parker: that had been the beginning of it. He might have tried Higgins for the money, but sure Higgins never had anything for himself. A man with two establishments to keep up, of course he couldn't. . . .

He felt his great body again aching for the comfort of the public-house. The fog had begun to chill him and he wondered could he touch Pat in O'Neill's. He could not touch him for more than a bob—and a bob was no use. Yet he must get money somewhere or other: he had spent his last penny for the g.p. and soon it would be too late for getting money anywhere. Suddenly, as he was fingering his watch-chain, he thought of Terry Kelly's pawn-office in Fleet Street. That was the dart! Why didn't he think of it sooner?

He went through the narrow alley of Temple Bar quickly, muttering to himself that they could all go to hell because he was going to have a good night of it. The clerk in Terry Kelly's said *A crown!* but the consignor held out for six shillings; and in the end the six shillings was allowed him literally. He came out of the pawn-office joyfully, making a little cylinder of the coins between his thumb and fingers. In Westmoreland Street the footpaths were crowded with young men and women returning from business and ragged urchins ran here and there yelling out the names of the evening editions. The man passed through the crowd, looking on the spectacle generally with proud satisfaction and staring masterfully at the office-girls. His head was full of the noises of tram-gongs and swishing trolleys and his nose already sniffed the curling fumes of punch. As he walked on he preconsidered the terms in which he would narrate the incident to the boys:

"So, I just looked at him—coolly, you know, and looked at her. Then I looked back at him again—taking my time, you know. 'I don't think that that's a fair question to put to me,' says I."

Nosey Flynn was sitting up in his usual corner of Davy Byrne's and, when he heard the story, he stood Farrington a half-one, saying it was as smart a thing as ever he heard. Farrington stood a drink in his turn. After a while O'Halloran and Paddy Leonard came in and the story was repeated to them. O'Halloran stood tailors of malt, hot, all round and told the story of the retort he had made to the chief clerk when he was in Callan's of Fownes's Street; but, as the retort was after the manner of the liberal shepherds in the eclogues, he had to admit that it was not as clever as Farrington's retort. At this Farrington told the boys to polish off that and have another.

Just as they were naming their poisons who should come in but Higgins! Of course he had to join in with the others. The men asked him to give his version of it, and he did so with great vivacity for the sight of five small hot whiskies was very exhilarating. Everyone roared laughing when he showed the way in which Mr. Alleyne shook his fist in Farrington's face. Then he imitated Farrington, saying, *"And here was my nabs, as cool as you please,"* while Farrington looked at the company out of his heavy dirty eyes, smiling and at times drawing forth stray drops of liquor from his moustache with the aid of his lower lip.

When that round was over there was a pause. O'Halloran had money but neither of the other two seemed to have any; so the whole party left the shop somewhat regretfully. At the corner of Duke Street Higgins and Nosey Flynn bevelled off to the left while the other three turned back towards the city. Rain was drizzling down on the cold streets and, when they reached the Ballast Office, Farrington suggested the Scotch House. The bar was full of men and loud with the noise of tongues and glasses. The three men pushed past the whining matchsellers at the door and formed a little party at the corner of the counter. They began to exchange stories. Leonard introduced them to a young fellow named Weathers who was performing at the Tivoli as an acrobat and knockabout *artiste.* Farrington stood a drink all round. Weathers said he would take a small Irish and Apollinaris. Farrington, who had definite notions of what was what, asked the boys would they have an Apollinaris too; but the boys told Tim to make theirs hot. The talk became theatrical. O'Halloran stood a round and then Farrington stood another round, Weathers protesting that the hospitality was too Irish. He promised to get them in behind the scenes and introduce them to some nice girls. O'Halloran said that he and Leonard would go, but that Farrington wouldn't go because he was a married man; and Farrington's heavy dirty eyes leered at the company in token that he understood he was being chaffed. Weathers made them all have just one little tincture at his expense and promised to meet them later on at Mulligan's in Poolbeg Street.

When the Scotch House closed they went round to Mulligan's. They went into the parlour at the back and O'Halloran ordered small hot specials all round. They were all beginning to feel mellow. Farrington was just standing another round when Weathers came back. Much to Farrington's relief he drank a glass of bitter this time. Funds were getting low but they had enough to keep them going. Presently two young women with big hats and a young man in a check suit came in and sat at a table close by. Weathers saluted them and told the company that they were out of the Tivoli. Farrington's eyes wandered at every moment in the direction of one of the young women. There was something striking in her appearance. An immense scarf of peacock-blue muslin was wound round her hat and knotted in a great bow under her chin; and she wore bright yellow gloves, reaching to the elbow. Farrington gazed admiringly at the plump arm which she moved very often and with much grace; and when, after a little time, she answered his gaze he admired still more her large dark brown eyes. The oblique staring expression in them fascinated him. She glanced at him once or twice and, when the party was leaving the room, she brushed against his chair and said *"O, pardon!"* in a London accent. He watched her leave the room in the hope that she would look back at him, but he was disappointed. He cursed his want of money and cursed all the rounds he had stood, particularly to all the whiskies and Apollinaris which he had stood to Weathers. If there was one thing that he hated it was a sponge. He was so angry that he lost count of the conversation of his friends.

When Paddy Leonard called him he found that they were talking about feats of strength. Weathers was showing his biceps muscle to the company and boasting so much that the other two had called on Farrington to uphold the national honour. Farrington pulled up his sleeve accordingly and showed his biceps muscle to the company. The two arms were examined and compared and finally it was agreed to have a trial of strength. The table was cleared and the two men rested their elbows on it, clasping hands. When Paddy Leonard said *"Go!"* each was to try to bring down the other's hand on to the table. Farrington looked very serious and determined.

The trial began. After about thirty seconds Weathers brought his opponent's hand slowly down on to the table. Farrington's dark wine-coloured face flushed darker still with anger and humiliation at having been defeated by such a stripling.

"You're not to put the weight of your body behind it. Play fair," he said.

"Who's not playing fair?" said the other.

"Come on again. The two best out of three."

The trial began again. The veins stood out on Farrington's forehead, and the pallor of Weathers' complexion changed to peony. Their hands and arms trembled under the stress. After a long struggle Weathers again brought his opponent's hand slowly on to the table. There was a murmur of applause from the spectators. The curate, who was standing beside the table, nodded his red head towards the victor and said with stupid familiarity:

"Ah! that's the knack!"

"What the hell do you know about it?" said Farrington fiercely, turning on the man. "What do you put in your gab for?"

"Sh, sh!" said O'Halloran, observing the violent expression of Farrington's face. "Pony up, boys. We'll have just one little smahan more and then we'll be off."

A very sullen-faced man stood at the corner of O'Connell Bridge waiting for the little Sandymount tram to take him home. He was full of smouldering anger and revengefulness. He felt humiliated and discontented; he did not even feel drunk; and he had only twopence in his pocket. He cursed everything. He had done for himself in the office, pawned his watch, spent all his money; and he had not even got drunk. He began to feel thirsty again and he longed to be back again in the hot reeking public-house. He had lost his reputation as a strong man, having been defeated twice by a mere boy. His heart swelled with fury and, when he thought of the woman in the big hat who had brushed against him and said *Pardon!* his fury nearly choked him.

His tram let him down at Shelbourne Road and he steered his great body along in the shadow of the wall of the barracks. He loathed returning to his home. When he went in by the side-door he found the kitchen empty and the kitchen fire nearly out. He bawled upstairs:

"Ada! Ada!"

His wife was a little sharp-faced woman who bullied her husband when he was sober and was bullied by him when he was drunk. They had five children. A little boy came running down the stairs.

"Who is that?" said the man, peering through the darkness.

"Me, pa."

"Who are you? Charlie?"

"No, pa. Tom."

"Where's your mother?"

"She's out at the chapel."

"That's right. . . . Did she think of leaving any dinner for me?"

"Yes, pa. I—"

"Light the lamp. What do you mean by having the place in darkness? Are the other children in bed?"

The man sat down heavily on one of the chairs while the little boy lit the lamp. He began to mimic his son's flat accent, saying half to himself: *"At the chapel. At the chapel, if you please!"* When the lamp was lit he banged his fist on the table and shouted:

"What's for my dinner?"

"I'm going . . . to cook it, pa," said the little boy.

The man jumped up furiously and pointed to the fire.

"On that fire! You let the fire out! By God, I'll teach you to do that again!"

He took a step to the door and seized the walking-stick which was standing behind it.

"I'll teach you to let the fire out!" he said, rolling up his sleeve in order to give his arm free play.

The little boy cried *"O pa!"* and ran whimpering round the table, but the man followed him and caught him by the coat. The little boy looked about him wildly but, seeing no way of escape, fell upon his knees.

"Now, you'll let the fire out the next time!" said the man, striking at him vigorously with the stick. "Take that, you little whelp!"

The boy uttered a squeal of pain as the stick cut his thigh. He clasped his hands together in the air and his voice shook with fright.

"O, pa!" he cried. "Don't beat me, pa! And I'll . . . I'll say a *Hail Mary* for you. . . . I'll say a *Hail Mary* for you, pa, if you don't beat me. . . . I'll say a *Hail Mary*. . . ."

In writing about a story, as we have said, you must begin by stating a proposition, a thesis, that you intend to argue. If you are given a topic such as Farrington's character or the structure of "Counterparts," you cannot write well until you think out a statement that summarizes generally what you intend to say.

In the exercise that follows, you are given a thesis; your assignment is to argue it with specific references to the main scenes of the story.

EXERCISES

1. Write an essay in which your opening section is as follows: A story may progress by repeating a similar structure in each scene. In "Counterparts" the structure of each major scene is built on Farrington's frustrations and his reactions to them.

You should concentrate on major scenes. Since the key words in the statement are "frustrations" and "reactions," you should outline by listing what specifically frustrates Farrington and how he reacts in each instance. You are being specific when a reader can look at your notes and put his finger on the part of the story that you are talking about. A phrase like "the way he acts" is not specific; a phrase like his "dark wine-coloured face flushed darker still" is specific. But quotations alone are not enough; you should indicate the significance of Farrington's face flushing at this particular moment. That is, you need to state why you are making a specific reference.

Your next step is to organize your paper. That problem is an easy one here; you can discuss each of the three main scenes in the order in which they occur. You will need to give details of the story to make clear to your reader what it is that you are talking about. You will need transitional phrases: for example, "After this scene Farrington begins a round of the pubs"; your reader will then be able to follow your argument more easily.

Your paper will take on this outline:

1. Your opening statement (given in the assignment).
2. A description of the first major scene, with the emphasis on the frustrations faced by Farrington: his reactions to them.
3. His tour of the pubs and the further frustrations: his reactions to them.
4. His arrival home: his reactions.
5. Finally, you should conclude with some general remarks on the meaning of the story—what it shows about human behavior, about Farrington in particular, about people in general. For help in working out the theme, look up the word *scapegoat* in the dictionary.

Keep in mind that a paper on any one aspect of a story should relate that aspect to the total meaning of the story.

The story "Counterparts" is an interesting illustration of how the voice that tells the story can affect our attitude toward the leading character. We said earlier that art is selective; the writer chooses what he will tell us and how he will tell us. For every speech and gesture included or summarized, many are left out. So we can assume that an author by choosing words, speeches, actions, and scenes has become subjective; he has taken an attitude toward his material that shows how he feels. If the author describes a character, his choices of words ("He had a hanging face, dark wine-coloured, with fair eyebrows and moustache: his eyes bulged forward slightly and the whites of them were dirty") indicate his feelings about that character and will influence ours.

A writer may also tell us what a character is thinking, "He felt that he must slake his thirst in his throat." The result is that what at first glance may seem objective is in reality subjective.

2. Write an essay on the following problem. Though much of "Counterparts" seems to be told objectively, the author does at times tell us what is going on in Farrington's mind. Where are the more important revelations of what Farrington is thinking, and how do they influence our understanding of the story? How, too, does the author express an attitude toward Farrington by the choice of words in describing him or his actions?

Your notes should be placed under two headings: where the storyteller gets into Farrington's mind, and where he indicates an attitude toward Farrington through a choice of words. Then draft an opening statement that summarizes what you are going to discuss. One test of a good opening is whether someone finding your essay on the street would know what you had been asked to write about.

Begin with a phrase similar to "In 'Counterparts' James Joyce expresses an attitude toward Farrington in two major ways." Then go on to explain what the two ways are. You may discuss each in turn. Implied in the question, of course, is the assumption that you will sum up for the reader what attitude the voice is taking toward Farrington.

3. Write an essay on the following problem. One of the tests of a story is whether the ending grows logically out of the previous action of the story. How is the final scene of "Counterparts" related to the earlier scenes?

4. Write an essay on the following question. In what ways do minor characters contribute to our understanding of Farrington?

Center your discussion on the most important minor characters, describing the ways in which they react with Farrington and what those interactions reveal about his character.

2

POETRY

READING AND UNDERSTANDING POETRY

When we return from a vacation we may have photographs to show our friends as a way of saying, "This is what it was like." A poem, too, re-creates an experience. A snapshot can show us a scene; a poem can show us the poet's thoughts about that scene. A poem works by relating the meanings of the words, by causing their sounds to echo one another, by creating imaginative images. This combination of meaning, sound, and image re-creates the poet's experience and evokes an emotional reaction from the reader. It can help the reader to see a common incident in a new or uncommon way.

The subject matter of poetry can be found in everything that interests the human mind. One volume of modern poetry includes such a variety of subjects as a groundhog, an aerial bombardment, camping, the death of a bombing victim, a dial tone, a campus on a hill. But the subject of a poem is only part of the meaning. The poet often uses a particular incident to make a larger statement on ideas, such as love, war, joy, sadness, heroism, fate, beauty, justice, or patriotism. The central topic of the poem is its *theme*, an abstract idea that is illustrated concretely in the subject of the poem.

In learning what the poet thinks, in seeing how he responds to an experience that may be similar to one we have known, we sharpen and deepen our own concept of the meaning of life and our understanding of experiences common to all men.

Reading poetry is the most exacting test of a person's ability to read, and it is an exercise in slow reading. The compression of meaning in a poem makes words perform like fireworks; new meanings will keep opening up if the reader gives his full attention to how the words interact. No good poem will yield its pattern of sound and meaning if it is read only once or twice. On the seventh reading, perhaps, one may begin to understand the poem if one asks the right questions.

A poem presents a dramatic situation. It is told by a speaking voice that is not necessarily the voice of the poet, even when he speaks as "I." Often the poet sets up a character whose voice dramatizes what is on the poet's mind. The poet may address a particular person. Dylan Thomas wrote of his father's dying, and the opening stanza of the poem reads:

> Do not go gentle into that good night,
> Old age should burn and rave at the close of day;
> Rage, rage against the dying of the light.

Here, as the poet compares the coming of death with night and darkness, he addresses himself directly to the dying man, asking that he fight back against death. Though the audience (listener) the poem is directed to is the poet's father, the reader himself is also part of the audience, and the poet's thought applies to him too.

Looking closely at a modern poem can help us to see how we might read and write about such a work.

LUNCH ON OMAHA BEACH — Bink Noll

The killers are killed, their violent rinds
Conveyed, and the beach is back to summer.
I eat sausage with bread. Full of ease, the sea
Makes the sound of cows chewing through high grass.

They're deposited in government lawn
Set with nine thousand decencies of stone
To wet the eye, shake the heart, and lose
Each name in a catalog of graven names.

They are wasted in the blank of herohood.
They are dead to fondness and paradox.
They're all the same. In the field of lawn
Above the beach, they're put away the same.

They should be left exactly here below where
Death's great bronze mares shook earth and bloodied
  them,
Where violence of noise isolated each boy
In the body of his scream, and dropped him.

No worn Norman hill should be scarred and smoothed
To suit officials' tidy thoughts for graveyards
But the wreckage left, shrinking in rust and rags
And carrion to dust or tumuli.

To honor my thoughts against shrines, to find
The beast who naked wakes in us and walks
In flags, to watch the color of his day
I spill my last Bordeaux into the sand.

Watching, I wonder at the white quiet,
The fields of butter cows, my countrymen
Come to study battle maps, blue peasants
Still moving back and forth, the day's soft sea.

We can begin with the explicit meaning of the poem. The poet is protesting the results and the causes of war by having the speaker in the poem talk about the fact that when the ugly signs of war are cleaned up, we may too easily forget the evil of it all. The speaker is picnicking on a beach in France where the Allied armies had landed under heavy bombardment on D-Day, June 1944, to carry out the invasion of Europe. He remembers what happened there ("The killers are killed") and recalls that the soldiers' bodies have been buried in an official cemetery. They should, he thinks, have been left on the beach where they had been killed ("the wreckage left"), instead of being tidily put away. To "honor" his beliefs against "shrines," he pours some wine on the beach. This also reminds him of the evil spirit that lurks in all of us, a spirit that can be stirred up through patriotism ("In flags"). Now he looks at the peaceful scene of the present and wonders why men fight each other.

In developing this explicit meaning, we should check the

dictionary meanings of any words that we are unsure of, such as *rind:* the skin of a fruit; *mares:* female horses (but *mares* also once meant goblins who caused nightmares); *carrion:* dead flesh; *tumuli:* artificial mounds; *Bordeaux:* a French red wine from the province of Bordeaux.

After we clarify the explicit, or apparent, meaning of the poem, we should then describe some of its other characteristics. This poem is made up of seven stanzas of four lines each. There is no rhyme to tie ideas together, but for the most part each stanza contains a major thought in the development of the poem. The lines are written in free verse, in which there is no regular beat, but only the rhythm of the speaking voice. The poem consists mostly of a series of images of sound, taste, sight, and feeling that bring us closer to the reality of the effects of war than would a general statement ("I am against war"). Beyond these obvious qualities of the poem, we should relate the form of the poem to the implied meanings, those that may not be quite as apparent as those explicit meanings developed earlier.

The pattern of the poem is based on contrasts: the past and the present, the cemetery and the beach, the dead and the living, war and peace. These contrasts with their interrelationships of meaning can help us understand the poem.

Now we can begin an explication of the poem by looking more carefully at the words, the *diction*, and their implications. Most of the words are concrete; abstractions (like "herohood," "fondness," and "paradox") are minimized. The bodies of the dead are compared to "violent rinds," suggesting the twisted torsos of those who died in battle as well as the dryness of death. The bodies have been "conveyed" (the rhythm emphasizes the word), a blunt understatement. "Summer" is used literally, but also suggests the idea of peace. In contrast to the past scenes of death is the peaceful picnic scene.

In the second stanza, the understatement of "deposited in government lawn" (the cemetery), under "decencies" (grave markers), indicates the poet's growing anger at the thought of so many men lost in the great mass. This anger mounts in the third stanza, in "wasted" and "blank"; men that cannot be considered heroes because they are so many—faceless and nameless.

In the fourth stanza, the moment of death is compressed into the metaphor of "bronze mares," an allusion, perhaps, to the Apocalypse, where war is a horseman, but also, through the language of comparison, a reference to the metal guns and tanks that

> isolated each boy
> In the body of his scream, and dropped him.

We should be forced to remember this carnage, not through "graveyards," but by the leaving of the "wreckage," the "rust and rags/ And carrion."

In the sixth stanza, the speaker argues against "shrines," and reminds himself of the evil beast that "wakes in us and walks/ In flags." The assumption here is that people are stirred to these terrible acts of war by a false, flag-waving patriotism that overcomes good sense. To emphasize the evil of killing, the speaker marks "the color of his [the beast's] day" by pouring wine on the beach. There are several levels of meaning here: Bordeaux is suitable for a French beach, the wine is the color of blood, and the pouring of wine suggests a religious act. All these meanings work into the deliberate ambiguity of the phrase.

The color of the wine is tied into the images of the final stanza. The earlier red is joined here by white and blue, reminding us of the colors of the American flag. The poem ends in the present by the "day's soft sea," an ironic contrast to the war that is past.

A poem, then, is an act of speech that takes place in a particular setting on a particular occasion. It is spoken by the poet or by someone who acts for him, a persona. It speaks in a particular tone (joy, anger, sadness), and may be a cry of anger, a song of joy, a statement of protest, a profession of love. The poem has a structure, which may offer a series of related images. Those images may be direct representations of reality, or they may be figurative comparisons that show vividly what something or someone is like. Often the sentence patterns are involved, to make the best use of rhythm or to throw heavy emphasis on key words.

In discussing "Lunch on Omaha Beach," we looked first at what happens in the poem, its explicit meaning. Then we turned to a description of the poem: what it is; how it is put together. Such a discussion can include, when they are important, the poem's sound pattern, its rhymes, repetition and comparison of ideas, and its imagery.

Then we turned to the deeper meanings of the poem, its implied meanings. By looking at the total pattern of the poem, we saw how the various parts are related and how the ideas move in space and time through cause and effect. Allusions to past events, persons, or mythology were fitted to the meaning. Finally, we restated what we took to be the total meaning of the poem and made an abstract statement of its theme, which in an essay is stated at the beginning.

AVOIDING BAD RESPONSES TO A POEM

When you are writing about a poem, make sure that the total content of the poem remains your subject.

Don't rush your reading and assume that a poem such as "Lunch at Omaha Beach" is about cows eating on a government lawn or about the bad upkeep of a cemetery or about the joy of going on picnics.

Don't ignore the images. Try to visualize the scenes the words represent.

Don't let particular words in the poem set off stock responses in your own mind. Key words in a poem can trigger irrelevant responses in a reader. In Noll's poem, "killers" or "carrion" should be considered in the context in which the poet uses them.

Don't let the poem merely remind you of your own past experiences. If you do, you will begin writing about picnics you have attended, wine that you have spilled, or soldiers whom you have known.

Don't allow your paper to become an argument with the poet. If you write about what you think of war, patriotism, or heroism, you may be ignoring what the poet has written.

Don't let your ideas about what poetry should be influence your reading. You cannot judge poetry by whether it has a regular beat, by whether "June" rhymes with "moon," or by what you might think is a suitable subject for poetry.

Now let us look at a different type of poem, Shakespeare's seventy-third sonnet.

SONNET 73 **William Shakespeare**

That time of year thou mayst in me behold
When yellow leaves, or none, or few, do hang
Upon those boughs which shake against the cold,
Bare ruined choirs, where late the sweet birds sang.
In me thou see'st the twilight of such day
As after sunset fadeth in the west;
Which by and by black night doth take away,
Death's second self that seals up all in rest.
In me thou see'st the glowing of such fire,
That on the ashes of his youth doth lie,
As the deathbed whereon it must expire,
Consumed with that which it was nourished by.
This thou perceiv'st, which makes thy love more strong,
To love that well which thou must leave ere long.

The speaker is addressing his love and is commenting on his own old age and the approach of death. He compares the time, or stage, of his life to a tree in winter, to the setting of the sun and the coming of night, and to a fading fire. Since the person to whom the poem is addressed is aware of his growing age, her love will grow stronger because the two will be separated soon.

The poem is a sonnet (a fourteen-line poem), composed here of four sentences: three are four lines long, and the concluding sentence is in the form of a couplet. Each of the first three sentences contains one major image, and the final statement is a general one that ties together the meanings of the previous images. This division of meaning is reinforced by the rhyme scheme—*a b a b c d c d e f e f g g;* each letter standing for a similar rhyming sound at the end of each line.

The rhythm of the poem is for the most part iambic pentameter, an unstressed sound followed by a stressed one, repeated five times per line.

˘ ʹ ˘ ʹ ˘ ʹ ˘ ʹ ˘ ʹ
That time of life thou mayst in me behold

The first variation in the rhythm comes in line 4, where a stress falls on "bare," where we had expected an unstressed sound.

> Bare ruined choirs, where late the sweet birds sang

And in line 8, Shakespeare throws the stress on "death."

> Death's second self, that seals up all the rest

Again, in line 11, the poet varies the stress to accent the idea of death.

> As the deathbed whereon it must expire

Finally, line 13 begins with the stress on "this." The effect of irregular accents in an otherwise regular beat is to throw the stress on key words in the poem. Since the meaning of the poem revolves around the thoughts of bareness and death, the sound and sense mesh perfectly as those key words are driven home by the stresses, as well as that put on the summarizing "this."

In addition, the sounds of the words contribute to the melody and emphasis, as vowels and consonants echo one another. In most cases that echo draws attention to particular words in the poem. Two main techniques are used to relate sound and meaning.

Assonance is the repetition of vowel sounds; we hear the echo of an a sound in the first sentence, in "mayst," "shake," "bare," and "late." In line 8, where the poet has placed two heavy stresses at the beginning of the line, he further underlines the meaning with the repeated e sound in "death's second self." In the same line, the sound occurs again in "rest."

The second technique is the use of *alliteration*, the repetition of initial sounds of words. In line 7, the repetition of the *b* in "by and by black night," combined with the change in the stress pattern, throws great emphasis on "black."

> Which by and by black night doth take away.

And looking back at line 8, note the repetition of the s sound. The words that get the strongest emphasis in the poem are "bare," "black," "death's second self," "deathbed," all related to the theme, and then the word "this."

The speaker is comparing his own age to a cold time of the year. The first image is that of trees with faded "yellow" leaves, or bare branches ("none"). No longer do birds sing in their "boughs" as they would in spring, when the world is young. Those branches are compared to "bare ruined choirs," the galleries of a ruined church. We are reminded of a church service and a graveyard. The repeated phrase "in me" introduces the second and parallel image, the approach of darkness in the day. The sentence progresses in time, from "twilight" to "sunset" to "black night." The night is compared to "Death's second self," a suggestion of death as being like a person who "seals up all in rest." "In me" is used again to introduce the third image, that of a fading fire. Again the image moves in time from "glowing" fire to "ashes" to its "death-bed."

The three images are related in that they all deal with the passing of time and so illustrate a major theme of the poem. In turn, they deal with the end of the year, the end of a day, the fading of a fire. Each image suggests the end of life: cold and silence, darkness and sealing up, ashes and death; and the last image has a sense of finality. There is also a movement in space in the relation of the images from outdoors to indoors, a sense of closing in. All are images of change.

Poetry, then, is usually a dramatic statement in which the writer recalls an experience and gives us an imagined re-vision of how it affected him. He interprets the action, giving it significance. His vision unfolds in the structure of the poem and the order of ideas.

Now we can turn to the ways by which a poet gets his effects and by which the reader interprets those effects.

DICTION

The speaker describes his experience in words, the diction of the poem. The first distinction that we make here is between the denotation and the connotation of a word. The former term applies to the specific meaning of a word; the latter to what the word suggests. The connotation of a word is important to a poet because it allows him to evoke an emotional response from a reader.

An emotionally charged word (another way of talking about connotation) may be used by politicians to arouse emotions of affection or hostility in their audiences. Such words as "radical," "snob," "bigot," "communist," "patriot" will arouse the emotions of an audience favorably or unfavorably toward the subject because of past experiences that are recalled by the use of the words. Advertisers give certain names to their products—Mustang, Tide, Cobra, Jaguar, Grand Prix—because of the emotional associations of the words. When the poet uses words for their connotative values, he, too, expects the reader to bring an active imagination to the associations that attach themselves to the words.

Even selecting the denotation of a word is not a simple matter. A reader must first be aware of all the dictionary meanings of a word, but which meaning to choose depends on the relation of that word to the other words in the selection, on the context. Context, then, controls the meaning of a word and sometimes suggests a new meaning; a poet often uses common words in an uncommon way. In the opening lines of "The Groundhog," Richard Eberhart says,

> In June, amid the golden fields,
> I saw a groundhog lying dead.
> Dead lay he; my senses shook,
> And mind outshot our naked frailty.

To consider mainly the problems of denotative meaning, remembering that it is impossible in reading poetry to completely omit connotation, look at the words "Dead" (line 3), "shook," "outshot," and "naked." "Dead" may be repeated to indicate that the animal is truly dead, not just playing at being dead (like an opossum). "Outshot," to judge by the context, means shooting beyond, seeing the limits of life. Putting a word like "naked" along with "frailty" is unusual. From all these considerations, we might conclude that the death of the groundhog in "golden fields" (the time of fruition and harvest) reminds the speaker that death may come to us at any time; we are "naked" in the sense of being unprotected from our fate.

Words, then, must be considered for both their qualities of denotation and connotation. Here is the opening stanza of Robert Frost's "To a Young Wretch," describing a boy who has cut down one of the speaker's trees at Christmas time.

> As gay for you to take your father's ax
> As take his gun—rod—to go hunting—fishing.
> You nick my spruce until its fiber cracks;
> It gives up standing straight and goes down swishing.
> You link an arm in its arm, and you lean
> Across the light snow homeward smelling green.

We know that "nick" means a slight cut or chip. As Frost uses the word, it suggests that the boy is not very powerful; he does not chop. He chips away until the tree falls. The dictionary does not help much with this idiom; we must see it in relation to other words. Frost uses the word "arm" twice. The first time it means the boy's actual arm, but "its arm" means the branch of the tree, which Frost is comparing to an arm. When we consider the connotation, referring to a branch as an arm seems to convey a friendly feeling toward the tree.

When Shakespeare, in a song called "Winter," says, "When all aloud the wind doth blow,/ And coughing drowns the parson's saw," we may be puzzled by what is meant by "saw." Does it mean that the parson is cutting wood? If we read on through the dictionary meanings of the word, we find that "saw" also means a familiar saying, a maxim. Then we see that the writer is creating an image of a parson droning on before his congregation, who in a cold church drown out his words with their coughing.

We must remember that no word by itself has a determinable meaning; we must find its meaning in the context of other words. Consider again the word "saw": He cut the wood with a *saw*. He *sawed* the air with his hand. His speech was full of old *saws*. I *saw* it happen. Each time the word is used, it has a different meaning; we determine what that meaning is by looking at the words that make up the verbal context in which the word is used.

We should not consider some words or sounds of words as sad or happy in themselves. What is suggested by sense or sound grows from the entire context of the poem. However, we can classify the words used in a particular poem. Words may be common or uncommon. If we list the words used in the first stanza of "Lunch on Omaha Beach" (the nouns, verbs, descriptive adjectives, and adverbs), we find that they are common words, those often used in ordinary writing: "killers," "killed," "violent rinds," "conveyed," "beach," "back," "summer," "eat," "sausage," "bread," "full ease," "sea," "makes," "sound," "cows," "chewing," "high," and "grass." With few exceptions (like "tumuli") the poem uses words known to most people. The same can be said for Shakespeare's sonnet.

A poet may also use a high proportion of more unusual words, such as in the first four lines of John Keats's "To Sleep."

> O soft embalmer of the still midnight,
>   Shutting, with careful fingers and benign,
> Our gloom-pleas'd eyes, embowered from the light,
>   Enshaded in forgetfulness divine;

"Embalmer," "benign," "gloom-pleas'd," "embowered," and "enshaded" are not likely to be used by an ordinary speaker. The effect of such words is to create a solemn and elevated tone. When a poet uses simple words, as Frost does, he seems to be speaking directly and intimately to us. The choice that the author makes between common and uncommon words is part of his style. It also affects the way in which a poem is read aloud—its tone.

A characteristic of modern poetry is the use of common words in uncommon ways. In "Lunch on Omaha Beach," Noll uses, for example, "violent rinds," "decencies of stone," "blank of herohood," "walks in flags," "butter cows," and "blue peasants." By doing this, he not only creates a memorable phrase, but compresses a good deal of meaning into a brief phrase.

In the first discussion of Noll's poem, we pointed out the distinction between concrete words—those that describe something that actually exists and can be experienced through the senses, like "scream," "graveyards," and "rags"—and abstract words—those that convey ideas and feelings, like "herohood," "fondness," and "paradox." A poet is most concerned with concrete diction, but the balance between concrete and abstract is another aspect of his style.

EXERCISE

Read the following poem and consider the meanings of the words "rend," "open," "tatters," "thick," "into," "presses up," and "plow" as they are used in the poem. Be sure that you pay attention to what the words suggest about the heat. One useful device is to consider how the poem would be changed if different words were substituted at any point; for example, "slice" instead of "rend."

HEAT

H. D.

O wind, rend open the heat,
cut apart the heat,
rend it to tatters.

Fruit cannot drop
through this thick air—
that presses up and blunts
the points of pears
and rounds the grapes.

Cut the heat—
plow through it,
turning it on either side
of your path.

Now write a paragraph demonstrating how the diction in the poem gives a sense of oppressive heat. First list the key words mentioned above. After each, write one or two ideas suggested by the word. For example:

Words	Suggestions
rend open	the air is so thick that it must be torn apart by the wind

An opening sentence or two for the paragraph should resemble the following:

The diction in "Heat" by H.D. suggests oppressively warm air. The poet asks the wind to "rend open the heat."

Your paragraph can then describe what is suggested by the words "rend open" and can continue by describing the uses of the other key words.

What has been said about the denotations and connotations of words can be further illustrated by the following poem:

BASE DETAILS **Siegfried Sassoon**

If I were fierce, and bald, and short of breath,
  I'd live with scarlet Majors at the Base,
And speed glum heroes up the line to death.
  You'd see me with my puffy petulant face,
Guzzling and gulping in the best hotel,
  Reading the Roll of Honor. "Poor young chap,"
I'd say—"I used to know his father well;
  Yes, we've lost heavily in this last scrap."
And when the war is done and youth stone dead,
  I'd toddle safely home and die—in bed.

Assume that you have been assigned an essay on the diction of "Base Details." Consider what can be said about the topic by asking questions. What is the subject being discussed? The poem is obviously an attack on war; more particularly it expresses the feelings of a soldier toward his officers. How does the diction suggest the speaker's attitude? In preparing an answer, list the words that have strong connotative meanings and in another column state what those words suggest.

MAKING NOTES ON THE DICTION OF THE POEM

Words	Suggestions
base	military base; also suggests a meaning of morally low and contemptible
details	military mission, but also minor matters
scarlet	color of dress uniform of British officers; also the color of blood
fierce, and bald, and short of breath puffy petulant face guzzling and gulping	fierce is sarcastic, to suggest its opposite. The majors are out of shape from drinking and eating too much
scrap	understatement suggests a minor fight, as opposed to a battle in which people die
toddle safely home and die—in bed	safety of officers contrasted with "youth stone dead"

THE THESIS STATEMENT

The speaker in the poem is an ordinary soldier who says that his life would be different if he were a major, or any officer. He sees an ironic contrast between the soldiers who die in battle and the officers who stay behind the lines. His attitude of bitterness toward the "scarlet Majors," and thus toward the war, is suggested by his choice of words. The thesis statement could then read:

In "Base Details," Siegfried Sassoon reveals through his diction a bitterness toward the fact that young men die in wars while the officers live safely behind the lines.

WRITING THE ESSAY

With one exception the ideas can be discussed in the order that they are presented in the poem. The double meaning of the title can be referred to at the end of the essay, when the deliberate ambiguity becomes apparent. The notes can be organized into an essay like the following:

The Diction of "Base Details"

Old men make and run wars; young men fight and die in them. In "Base Details," Siegfried Sassoon reveals through his diction a bitterness toward the fact that young men die in wars while the officers live safely behind the lines. The speaker in the poem is an ordinary soldier talking about the majors at the army base. By pretending what he would be like if he were an officer, he condemns war.

Through his choice of words, the soldier expresses an attitude of contempt for the officers behind the lines who "speed glum heroes up the line to death." He speaks with sarcasm of their fierceness and goes on to describe them as "bald, and short of breath." If he were a major, he, too, would have a "puffy petulant face,/Guzzling and gulping in the best hotel." The connotations of these words suggest men who are overweight and out of shape from drinking and eating too much. The reference to "scarlet Majors" recalls the red dress-uniforms of British officers and the color of blood.

The speaker then goes on to describe the attitude toward soldiers that is held by the officers. One speaks of losing many men in "this last scrap." The understatement of that last word contrasts sharply with the mention in the same line of a heavy loss in battle. In the last two lines of the poem, a further contrast is set up between "youth stone dead" and the officer who will "toddle safely home and die—in bed."

When the entire poem is read, the title becomes ambiguous. The apparent meaning refers to the details of a military base. But "base" can also mean low and contemptible. "Detail" also has two meanings. It can mean a detachment of men sent out on a particular mission—"speed glum heroes up the line"—but it can also mean a minor matter, as if sending people off to die is not important to the officers. So the apparent meaning that we see as we begin reading turns into a second meaning when we finish reading the poem.

The diction, then, makes a comment on the theme of the poem: old men who direct wars at a safe distance behind the lines seem to have little understanding of what it means to die in battle and appear on "the Roll of Honor."

EXERCISE

Read the next poem carefully and examine the comments that follow it. Then write an essay comparing the poem with "Base Details" in its attitude toward war. Remember that in comparing, you should show similarities and differences.

I HAVE A RENDEZVOUS WITH DEATH — Alan Seeger

I have a rendezvous with Death
At some disputed barricade,
When Spring comes back with rustling shade
And apple-blossoms fill the air—
I have a rendezvous with Death
When Spring brings back blue days and fair.
It may be he shall take my hand
And lead me into his dark land
And close my eyes and quench my breath—
It may be I shall pass him still.
I have a rendezvous with Death
On some scarred slope of battered hill,
When Spring comes round again this year
And the first meadow-flowers appear.

God knows 'twere better to be deep
Pillowed in silk and scented down,
Where love throbs out in blissful sleep,
Pulse nigh to pulse, and breath to breath,
Where hushed awakenings are dear . . .
But I've a rendezvous with Death
At midnight in some flaming town;
When Spring trips north again this year,
And I to my pledged word am true,
I shall not fail that rendezvous.

The voice in this poem is that of a soldier who feels that he may be about to die in battle. He takes a romantic view of this duty, although love has more appeal for him than war. An ironic contrast is made between his "rendezvous with Death" and the coming of spring, ordinarily a time of rebirth. In spite of these thoughts, he will be true to his "pledged word" and is ready to die.

The romantic attitude of "I Have a Rendezvous with Death" can be seen clearly if the key words are listed with the ideas that they suggest.

Words	**Suggested Ideas**
rendezvous	a romantic meeting
disputed barricade	a pleasant way of speaking of a battle
rustling shade . . . apple blossoms . . . blue days and fair	beauty of coming spring
take my hand/And lead me into his dark land	death will come quietly and pleasantly
Pillowed in silk and scented down	a longing for the joys of love
Where love throbs out . . . hushed awakenings	
pledged word	connects dying in battle with honor

Before you write, make notes in answer to the following questions: What is the explicit meaning of each poem? What ideas and associations are suggested by the key words in each? (You may use those suggested in the text.) What attitude does each poem take toward death in war?

If you look at the questions you have asked and the resultant notes, they suggest the following outline:

1. Meaning of the poem
2. Ideas and associations of key words
3. Attitude toward war

You now have several obvious organizational patterns. You could take one poem at a time and discuss each in relation to these three headings, or you could compare each poem under the appropriate heading. You could take the meaning in one poem and compare it with the meaning of the other; you could then compare the ideas and associations of key words in one poem with those in the other; and finally, you could discuss the attitude toward war in one poem with the attitude in the other.

IMAGERY

We learn about the world through our senses: seeing a sunrise, feeling a cold wind, hearing the song of a bird, smelling the exhaust of a car, tasting hot coffee. As we retain these sensory impressions in our minds, we accumulate knowledge, and at the same time build up a stock of emotional attitudes toward those experiences.

Sensory stimulation can remind us of other similar experiences that we thought were forgotten: a strain of music may recall a dance; a whiff of perfume, a particular girl; a sight of a rose in a vase, a garden we once knew. It is this complex psychological process that the poet is drawing on when he creates images, concrete words that suggest reality by appealing to our senses. He is, in a way, slipping words into our minds; and we, like slide projectors, project a scene that serves the purpose of the poem. If we bring a creative imagination to the reading, our senses will recapture similar occasions. This is not to suggest that our experience can ever be identical to that of the poet, but if we read,

> I wandered lonely as a cloud
> That floats on high o'er vales and hills,
> When all at once I saw a crowd, a host of golden daffodils;
> Beside the lake, beneath the trees,
> Fluttering and dancing in the breeze.
>
> Wordsworth, "The Daffodils"

we will visualize scenes with clouds, hills, trees, lakes, and daffodils that we have seen. And we may remember a time when we were walking in the country and came upon a field of flowers. Then we can to some extent share the feeling of the poet.

Our vague and general view of the moon may be seen in a new way after we read:

> The moon is a ghostly galleon tossed upon cloudy seas,
>
> Noyes, "The Highwayman"

Or we may have a new feeling of a cold wind:

> . . . where the wind's like a whetted knife;
>
> Masefield, "Sea Fever"

Or we may get a new sense of the evening song of a bird:

> The pale purple even
> Melts around thy flight;
> Like a star of Heaven,
> In the broad daylight
> Thou art unseen, but yet I hear thy shrill delight,
>
> Shelley, "To a Skylark"

Or a new view of early morning:

> Night's candles are burnt out, and jocund day
> Stands tiptoe on the misty mountain tops.
>
> Shakespeare, *Romeo and Juliet*

Through these images, a poet shares his experience with the reader. In another sense, a poet is often painting a picture in words, and he suggests colors, sounds, and movement. He is capturing the quality of a moment and making it vivid. If we read enough poetry, we may become more aware of the world around us and more aware of our relationship to it.

EXERCISE

The ways in which voice, diction, image, and theme can work together to create a poem can be seen in the following poem:

NEUTRAL TONES — Thomas Hardy

We stood by a pond that winter day,
And the sun was white, as though chidden of God,
And a few leaves lay on the starving sod;
—They had fallen from an ash, and were gray.

Your eyes on me were as eyes that rove
Over tedious riddles of years ago;
And some words played between us to and fro
  On which lost the more by our love.

The smile on your mouth was the deadest thing
Alive enough to have strength to die;
And a grin of bitterness swept thereby
  Like an ominous bird a-wing. . . .

Since then, keen lessons that love deceives,
And wrings with wrong, have shaped to me
Your face, and the God-curst sun, and a tree,
  And a pond edged with grayish leaves.

The speaker in the poem is one of two people at the end of a love affair who are saying good-by. There is no evidence as to whether the speaker is a man or a woman; to make the discussion easier, we will assume that the speaker is a man addressing a woman. The first three stanzas, each containing a single sentence, are recalled from the past. The stanzas, in turn, deal with the scene of the meeting, the girl's eyes, and her smile.

The action in the poem is slight: the couple stand, look into one another's eyes, and exchange a few meaningless words ("words played between us to and fro"). One smiles, and the ellipsis (. . .) at the end of the third stanza indicates something omitted and suggests that more could have been said but would not have changed the situation.

In the fourth stanza, the speaker thinks back ("Since then") to the moment described in the first three stanzas. Further experiences ("keen lessons") have shown him that "love deceives" and can cause great sorrow ("wrings [his heart] with wrong"). These further experiences bring the speaker to recall the face of his former love and the place where they said good-by.

The poet gets his emotional effect largely through his choice of images and diction. The major images are those of the pond and its setting, the eyes, and the smile. We see the images through the speaker's eyes, and the connotations of the words reflect his mood and thoughts.

EXERCISE

Now write an essay on the poem, stating in the first paragraph your own version of what the poem is about. Then go on to show how the poet's choices of words and images contribute to the meaning of the poem. Note especially the use of color.

ANALYSIS OF A POEM

How a series of images will work together to form the total effect of a poem can be seen in the discussion of the following poem from *Understanding Poetry* by Cleanth Brooks and Robert Penn Warren.

TO AN ATHLETE DYING YOUNG — A. E. Housman

The time you won your town the race
We chaired you through the market-place;
Man and boy stood cheering by,
And home we brought you shoulder-high.

Today, the road all runners come,
Shoulder-high we bring you home,
And set you at your threshold down,
Townsman of a stiller town.

Smart lad, to slip betimes away
From fields where glory does not stay
And early though the laurel grows
It withers quicker than the rose.

Eyes the shady night has shut
Cannot see the record cut,
And silence sounds no worse than cheers
After earth has stopped the ears:

Now you will not swell the rout
Of lads that wore their honors out,
Runners whom renown outran
And the name died before the man.

So set, before its echoes fade,
The fleet foot on the sill of shade,
And hold to the low lintel up
The still-defended challenge-cup.

And round that early-laureled head
Will flock to gaze the strengthless dead,
And find unwithered on its curls
The garland briefer than a girl's.

In this poem the poet states a paradox: * namely, that the early death of the young athlete is a matter for congratulation rather than for sorrow. This is the real theme of the poem. But we should hardly be impressed with the bare statement that it is better to die young rather than old, and even the startling quality of the statement would awaken interest for only a moment. The poet has known better than to state the matter baldly therefore he has arranged a little dramatic framework for the statement. In a familiar, almost conversational tone—"Smart lad"—he addresses his congratulations to the young man who is dead; and more than that, he uses the images which are associated with the young man's athletic achievements to describe his death. Indeed, the statement implied by the imagery of the poem is that the young runner has, in dying, won his race again—he has beaten his competitors to the final goal of them all, death.

Notice, for example, that the funeral is treated exactly as if it were a triumph for the young runner celebrated by his friends. On the day on which he won the race for his town, his friends made a chair for him of their hands and carried him home shoulder-high in triumph. Now on the day of his funeral, they carry him "shoulder-high" again,

* paradox: a statement which seems to be contradictory or absurd, but may be actually true.

and they bring him "home." "Smart lad," the poet then calls him, as if he had just finished running a heady race.

The reasons for saying this follow: it is better to die at the prime than to witness one's records broken by some one else. But the poet does not relax his hold on concrete details in making this statement. The laurel, symbol of fame, withers even quicker than does the rose, emblem of beauty. Eyes closed in death cannot see the record broken; to ears stopped with earth, the silence rings as loud as the air filled with cheering. And now the poet returns to the dominant figure of the race. Fame has a habit of outrunning the fastest runner and leaving him behind; the young athlete has not been outrun by his renown.

The figure is developed further in the sixth stanza. The brink of the grave is "the sill of shade" on which the young man has just placed his fleet foot, and the edge of the grave is the "low lintel" up to which the boy holds the "still defended challenge cup." The paradoxes here are especially rich. We think of death as being opposed in every regard to fleetness, and its inertia as incapable of defending anything. Yet by the reasoning which has preceded this stanza, the foot of the dead youth *is* fleet in death—only in death can he hold his challenge-cup still defended. Others will not be able to wrest it from him. The passage is a fine example of the poet's ability to put things which we ordinarily think of as quite unrelated, or even opposed to each other, into a pattern which gives a meaningful relation where one had not been seen before.

The last stanza exhibits also a fine effect which the poet has prepared for. The stanza catches up the contrast between the laurel and the rose already made in the third stanza. The connection is hinted at in the phrase "early-laureled head." Fame perishes even more quickly than beauty—the garland of laurel withers even faster than the garland of roses a girl might be supposed to wear. We think of a young girl dead in the first flush of her beauty as an object of pathos, and at the same time think of her as having achieved a sort of triumph at having brought all her beauty untarnished with her into the grave. The poet wishes to get, and does get, something of the same effect for the athlete, and he gets it by suggesting the comparison.

EXERCISE

Read this poem and the comments that follow it. To understand the poem, you must know the meanings of all the words: especially "lute," "render," "dirges," "knell," "bewailest," "frailty," and "bier."

LINES: WHEN THE LAMP IS SHATTERED

Percy Bysshe Shelley

1

When the lamp is shattered
The light in the dust lies dead—
When the cloud is scattered
The rainbow's glory is shed.
When the lute is broken,
Sweet tones are remembered not;
When the lips have spoken,
Loved accents are soon forgot.

2

As music and splendor
Survive not the lamp and the lute,
The heart's echoes render
No song when the spirit is mute—
No song but sad dirges,
Like the wind through a ruined cell,
Or the mournful surges
That ring the dead seaman's knell.

3

When hearts have once mingled
Love first leaves the well-built nest;
The weak one is singled
To endure what it once possessed.
O Love! who bewailest
The frailty of all things here,
Why choose you the frailest,
For your cradle, your home, and your bier?

4

Its passions will rock thee
As the storms rock the ravens on high;
Bright reason will mock thee,
Like the sun from a wintry sky.
From thy nest every rafter
Will rot, and thine eagle home
Leave thee naked to laughter,
When leaves fall and cold winds come.

Consider first the images of broken things in the first stanza, the lamp, clouds, and lute, and the image of forgotten words.

The second stanza contains a comparison. As the music and the splendor do not survive the breaking (of two images, the lute and the lamp, repeated from the first stanza), so too do the "heart's echoes" become "mute" when they are not moved by a "spirit." In the last half of the stanza, the "song" becomes a "dirge" and is compared to the images of "wind" and the "ring" of a bell buoy moved by the "surges" (the waves of the sea). What words in the second stanza are related to ideas in the first stanza? What ideas in the first stanza are made more specific in the second?

In the third stanza, "mingled" here means being in love, and being in love is compared to living in a "well-built nest." When love leaves (breaks up), the weaker of the couple must suffer more. Then the poet addresses love directly on the frailty of things "here" (on earth), and on why the effects live on in the frailer (Shelley says "frailest" for purposes of rhyme) of the two, who continues to suffer.

In the last stanza, "its" refers to love, or what is left of it, and "thee" is the one who continues to suffer (the frailer). What that person goes through after love has ended is described in a series of images: storms, reason as the sun, the nest (also called "thine eagle home"), and winter.

After you have worked out what you take to be the meaning of the whole poem, write an essay on what the poem is saying about the nature of love. Be sure that you include your ideas on what the various images and their connotations contribute to the poem's meaning.

THE LANGUAGE OF COMPARISON

Poetry draws on knowledge, emotion, and imagination. We acquire knowledge through our senses; we learn as we hear, touch, smell, taste, or see. We may learn about stones by seeing and feeling them and by hearing them clink together. We may see, touch, smell, and taste plants. Thereafter, our memory helps us retain the sensations. We also take on emotional attitudes toward our surroundings. Most people react differently toward a snake than toward a rabbit; toward a thunderstorm than a shower; toward a dandelion than a rose.

Imagination allows us to form mental representations of concrete objects, to "see" them when the objects are not present. When someone asks where we live, an image of a house or room may appear in our minds; then we try to put the vision into words. Through imagination we can recall a seashore, a busy street, a facial expression.

And so a poet, through his imagination, can create a situation for us. He can express a vision that becomes his poem. His method depends largely on concrete images, but often his language moves from literal (the dictionary meaning of the word) to metaphoric (the language of comparison). The poet's gift is the extent of his imagination, the power of representing vividly the details of a thing or a situation. The poet imitates nature in arousing our senses and forcing us to use them imaginatively.

Metaphoric language compresses language and thought; a great deal can be said and suggested in a word or brief phrase. The language of comparison is a common way of speaking: in news headlines—*Candidates woo upstate New York*; on the sports page—*The pitcher dusts off the batter*; in science—*The brain is like an electronic computer*; in slang—*Keep your cool*; in common sayings—*It's a long road that has no turning*. These are simple types of compression. A poet gets more ideas into his highly evocative comparisons.

But far more important than compression is imagination, a new way of looking at a common thing. The analogy of the poet not only brings a fresh, memorable quality to the writing, but also takes us far beyond the simple act of comparison. Emily Dickinson sees a snake, "The grass divides as with a comb"; Milton speaks of dawn as "the opening eyelids of the morn";

and William Collins writes, "The dewy fingers draw/ The gradual dusky veil."

One of the major difficulties in reading is that of knowing when language shifts from its literal meaning to its metaphoric meaning. Shakespeare speaks literally when he gives the impression of cold by adding up specific images in his poem "Winter."

When icicles hang by the wall
  And Dick the shepherd blows his nail,
And Tom bears logs into the hall,
  And milk comes frozen home in pail,
When blood is nipp'd, and ways be foul,
Then nightly sings the staring owl,
                                        Tu-who;
Tu-whit! tu-who—a merry note,
While greasy Joan doth keel the pot.

When all aloud the wind doth blow,
  And coughing drowns the parson's saw,
And birds sit brooding in the snow,
  And Marian's nose looks red and raw,
When roasted crabs hiss in the bowl,
Then nightly sings the staring owl,
                                        Tu-who;
Tu-whit, tu-who—a merry note,
While greasy Joan doth keel the pot.

We may have more difficulty in working out the language of metaphor, when the literal meaning is compared to a figurative one. In the first stanza of "The Wish" Abraham Cowley writes:

  Well then; I now do plainly see,
This busy world and I shall ne'er agree;
The very honey of all earthly joy
  Does of all meats the soonest cloy;
  And they, methinks, deserve my pity
Who for it can endure the stings,
The crowd, and buzz, and murmurings
  Of this great hive, the city.

After the direct statement of the first two lines, he goes on to compare people living in a city with bees living in a hive. The "honey" (gold or goods) that is the result of such living is not worth the "stings" (difficulties or hurts) of living in such crowded conditions that men become like a "hive" of bees. There is also the suggestion that the men, like the bees, are continually at work. The writer also alludes to the constant "buzz," the never-ending noise of the city. He then goes on, in the rest of the poem, to hope for a chance to live in the country.

The basis of metaphor is comparison: the literal concept being discussed (a city) is compared to something else (a hive) because the writer sees a resemblance between them. In the above stanza, then, "city" is the literal term; "hive" is the figurative term. Together they form a metaphor. Notice, too, that the comparison is extended to develop some of the characteristics of the hive that also apply to the city.

If the comparison is directly stated, by the use of *like, as, seems, appears, than, so,* we describe it with the word *simile*, a subdivision of metaphor. Here are examples:

Art is long, and Time is fleeting,
And our hearts, though stout and brave
Still, like muffled drums, are beating
Funeral marches to the grave.
Longfellow, "A Psalm of Life"

My heart is like a singing bird
Whose nest is in a watered shoot:
My heart is like an apple tree
Whose boughs are bent with thickset fruit;
C. Rossetti, "A Birthday"

In such cases, the things compared, heart and drums, heart and bird, heart and apple tree, are clearly stated and easily read. In a metaphor, however, the linking word (like, as, than) is omitted, though the two terms compared may be expressed. Wordsworth, in a short poem named by its opening line, compares a girl to a violet and then to a star, creating two metaphors.

She dwelt among the untrodden ways
Beside the springs of Dove,
A maid whom there were none to praise
And very few to love;

A violet by a mossy stone
  Half hidden from the eye!
—Fair as a star, when only one
  Is shining in the sky.

She lived unknown, and few could know
  When Lucy ceased to be;
But she is in her grave, and, oh,
  The difference to me!

Here, after literally describing the girl in the first stanza, the poet shifts to metaphoric images, stating that she is like a violet and a single star, reinforcing the ideas of beauty and loneliness.

A metaphor is created when a writer sees some common characteristic, between the literal concept (a girl) and a figurative one (a violet). The two things compared may be alike in their appearance:

The wild tulip, at the end of its tube, blows out its great red bell
Like a thin clear bubble of blood, for the children to pick and sell.

Browning, "Up at a Villa—Down in the City"

Or in what they do:

Music that gentlier on the spirit lies,
Than tired eyelids upon tired eyes;

Tennyson, "The Lotos-Eaters"

Or in how they make us feel:

Shall I compare thee to a summer's day?
Thou art more lovely and more temperate:

Shakespeare, Sonnet 18

A good metaphor will usually combine more than one type of comparison. In Wordsworth's metaphor, the girl does not look like a violet, but like that flower she does live in a remote place. It also evokes an emotion that we might feel in coming upon a beautiful thing.

Robert Burns uses all three of the above bases of comparison in the first stanza of "John Anderson My Jo":

John Anderson my jo,* John,
  When we were first acquent,
Your locks were like the raven,
  Your bonie brow was brent;
But now your brow is beld, John,
  Your locks are like the snaw;
But blessings on your frosty pow,
  John Anderson my jo!

John's hair is now white, looking like snow ("snaw"). Then too, black hair ("like the raven") may turn white as a person ages. The snow also suggests a feeling associated with winter, a common metaphor for the closing period of life.

In reading metaphors some questions are useful:

1. Is the passage literal or metaphoric?
2. What two things are being compared?
3. Which is the literal term and which is the figurative?
4. In what ways are the two things alike?
5. What does the metaphor mean literally?

Now read the following metaphors, each describing mountains:

The mountains they are silent folk,
  They stand afar—alone,
And the clouds that kiss their brows at night
  Hear neither sigh nor groan.
Each bears him in his ordered place
  As soldiers do, and bold and high
They fold their forests round their feet
  And bolster up the sky.

Garland, "The Mountains They Are Silent Folk"

Where the tall Rockies pasture with their
  heads down, white-spotted and streaked
  like piebald horses, sharp withers
And thunder-scarred shoulders against the sky,

* jo: joy

standing with their heads down,
the snow-manes blow in the wind;
But they will lift their heads and whinny
when the riders come, they will stamp
with their hooves and shake down the glaciers.

Jeffers, "Solstice"

We can outline the comparisons as follows:

Items compared by Garland

mountains	"silent folk"
How are they alike?	
stand alone in place	like soldiers
clouds cluster at peak	seem to kiss brows
forests at base	like blanket at feet
very high	seem to hold up the sky

Items compared by Jeffers

Rocky Mountains	"piebald horses"
How are they alike?	
snow-streaked	"white-spotted and streaked"
irregular, ragged peaks	"scarred shoulders" and "sharp withers"
sloping sides	like head-down horses
snowstorms	white manes
storm clouds gather	"riders come"
shapes seem to change	"lift their heads"
noises of storm	"whinny . . . stamp with their hooves"
glaciers move	seem to "shake down" the ice

Each writer creates a metaphor by comparing mountains on the basis of what they look like to him and on what they do. Yet each writer is also taking an emotional attitude toward his subject by what he chooses for his comparison. A reader of the first poem takes an attitude toward mountains that remind him of "folks" settling down for the night with a blanket over their feet. But he will have a different attitude toward an image of a piebald horse that stamps, whinnies, and shakes ice from the mountains.

EXERCISE

Using the above notes, write an essay analyzing the metaphors. Once you determine what the attitude of each writer is, make a list of key words taken from each selection that will support what you think. Put one list under the heading *Garland*, the other under *Jeffers*.

First write one or more opening sentences that state generally what your essay is about. Make it clear in your introduction that you are setting up a contrast. Then discuss each writer's attitude in separate paragraphs, using the order that you established in the introductory remarks. Support what you say by specific references taken from your lists. Give roughly equal space to each author.

SYMBOL

Closely related to the metaphor, and often difficult to distinguish from it, is the symbol. A symbol is an image of one thing that stands for another. It may be perceived through the senses, but it goes beyond them to convey another level of meaning. A cross, for example, evokes many associations with Christianity.

Some common symbols embody meanings that any experienced reader will recognize; constant use has made them clichés. The rising and setting sun can stand for birth and death or hope and despondency; so can spring and winter or the rise and fall of the tide. A road may represent life, with its ups and downs, its twists and turns, all expressing the changing fortunes of man. A person choosing between two roads may be making a decision that will affect his life. The growth and spread of a family may be represented by the branching of a tree; old age and death, by the withering and falling leaf. The "inconstant moon" has suggested to many writers the changing quality of love. The moon keeps changing its form as does the love between two people. A spring of water has been used as a symbol of strength; the arid land, of weakness and barrenness.

Though poets draw on this common body of ideas, they often create more private symbols that take their meanings from the contexts in which they are used. A figure of a person working in a field may stand for all those who spend their lives at menial jobs; a broken statue may gather a poet's thought on the brevity of fame; or a rose may suggest quick-fading beauty. A poet uses such symbols to stand for the cluster of ideas and feelings that are in his mind. The reader is expected to interpret the symbol according to how it relates to the meaning of the poem.

In using a metaphor, a poet is making an implied comparison of one term with another. In using a symbol, he is allowing an object to stand for, or to suggest, an idea. In the latter instance, the first term of the comparison is missing.

Edwin Markham saw a painting by Millet of a human figure bent over a hoe while working in a field. The picture seemed to symbolize all those who are hopelessly tied to hard labor. In "The Man with the Hoe" he wrote in part:

> Bowed by the weight of centuries he leans
> Upon his hoe and gazes on the ground,
> The emptiness of ages in his face,
> And on his back the burden of the world.
> Who made him dead to rapture and despair,
> A thing that grieves not and that never hopes,
> Stolid and stunned, a brother to the ox?
> Who loosened and let down this brutal jaw?
> Whose was the hand that slanted back this brow?
> Whose breath blew out the light within this brain?

Here the symbol is explained at some length.

In Edmund Waller's "Song," a rose is used as a symbol:

> Go, lovely rose!
> Tell her that wastes her time and me
> That now she knows,
> When I resemble* her to thee,
> How sweet and fair she seems to be.
>
> Tell her that's young,
> And shuns to have her graces spied,
> That hadst thou sprung
> In deserts, where no men abide,
> Thou must have uncommended died.

*resemble: liken

Small is the worth
Of beauty from the light retired;
Bid her come forth,
Suffer herself to be desired,
And not blush so to be admired.

Then die! that she
The common fate of all things rare
May read in thee;
How small a part of time they share
That are so wondrous sweet and fair!

The poet speaks to the rose as he sends it to his love. In the first stanza it stands for her beauty: "How sweet and fair she seems to be." The poet seems to be setting up a metaphor, but as he goes on, the rose takes on symbolic value. We learn that the shy girl, unlike the rose, does not want "to have her graces spied." If the rose had lived in a desert, unseen by man, its beauty would never have been praised. We are reminded that beauty should not be hidden, but admired. Then the rose should die as a reminder that "all things rare . . . sweet and fair" last only a short while. The girl should be more like the rose, available for the poet's admiration. In this poem, as in the quotation from Markham, the author gives the symbol and then elaborates on its meaning.

A more complex use of symbols occurs in William Blake's "The Sick Rose"; it is complex because we do not have enough context to settle on any exact meaning.

O Rose, thou art sick.
The invisible worm
That flies in the night
In the howling storm

Has found out thy bed
Of crimson joy,
And his dark secret love
Does thy life destroy.

The literal meaning here is that a rose has been attacked by a worm and is dying. If we consider the symbolic meanings of "rose" and "worm," what do we get from the poem? We need to make all the possible connections that we can between the specific meanings of the words, their grammatical relationships, and their emotional associations.

The poem operates largely through contrast. Traditionally a rose stands for a beautiful thing. A worm is connected with a snake as a symbol of evil (the Garden of Eden) and is thereby associated with Satan. The connotations of other key words help to support the contrast; "sick," "night," "howling storm," "dark secret love," and "destroy" all apply to the idea of evil in nature, as opposed to the "crimson joy."

The two major symbols suggest two sexes. The worm is male ("*his* dark secret love"), and we might guess that "thy life" refers to a woman. The rose is often used as a symbol of feminine beauty.

Some "invisible" evil, then, has destroyed some form of good —that much we can be sure of. To interpret the symbols beyond that, we must guess, but our guess should be based on the various interrelationships already pointed out.

Is the poem saying that good (the rose) can be corrupted by evil (the worm)? Or is it saying that illicit love (note "bed" and "secret love") is destructive?

Our thinking and asking questions about symbols show the way that we need to read beyond the literal meaning of a poem. Final answers are not always possible. Whatever interpretation we give to a symbol must fit the context of the poem.

EXERCISES

1. OZYMANDIAS — Percy Bysshe Shelley

I met a traveller from an antique land
Who said: Two vast and trunkless legs of stone
Stand in the desert . . . Near them, on the sand,
Half sunk, a shattered visage lies, whose frown,
And wrinkled lip, and sneer of cold command,
Tell that its sculptor well those passions read
Which yet survive, stamped on these lifeless things,
The hand that mocked them, and the heart that fed.*

*The hand of the sculptor who imitated them and the heart of the king that fed them.

And on the pedestal these words appear:
"My name is Ozymandias, king of kings:
Look on my works, ye Mighty, and despair!"
Nothing beside remains. Round the decay
Of that colossal wreck, boundless and bare
The lone and level sands stretch far away.

Write an essay on the meaning of "Ozymandias." First state the literal meaning of the poem and characterize Ozymandias. Then point out what the broken statue and its setting symbolize. Keep in mind that Ozymandias was an Egyptian tyrant, Ramses II, and the poem was published in 1817.

Begin with a statement like, " 'Ozymandias' is about . . ." Then answer the question, What is the literal meaning of the poem? In the second paragraph begin with a phrase such as, The broken statue symbolizes the idea of . . . Finally, state why you think the poem was relevant in 1817, given the rise of Napoleon. You may also be able to cite a more contemporary example of the poem's relevancy.

2. CROSSING THE BAR — Alfred, Lord Tennyson

Sunset and evening star,
  And one clear call for me!
And may there be no moaning of the bar,*
  When I put out to sea,

But such a tide as moving seems asleep,
  Too full for sound and foam,
When that which drew from out the boundless deep
  Turns again home.

Twilight and evening bell,
  And after that the dark!
And may there be no sadness of farewell,
  When I embark;

For though from out our bourne of Time and Place
  The flood may bear me far,
I hope to see my Pilot face to face
  When I have crossed the bar.

*bar: the sandbar that lies across the harbor-mouth except at high tide.

Write an essay on the use of symbols in this poem, pointing out how they relate to the meaning of death. Begin with a statement on the literal meaning: the poet is suggesting the idea of death by using the symbol of the sailing of a ship. Go on to show how the other symbols work by answering the following question: How does the poet make use of the images in nature, the coming of night, the tide and the sea, the implied movement of the ship, the pilot? Finally, point out what attitude the poet is taking toward death.

SOUND

A prose writer will use many of the devices mentioned so far, but the poet depends much more on the musical quality of his lines; thus poetry, beyond what it "says," affects us by its sounds. Its rhythms should give pleasure and heighten our attention; sometimes they may imitate the situation being described. Variations within a regular rhythm will emphasize the meaning of a word or phrase, calling it sharply to our attention.

Everyone is affected by rhythm. Children will chant meaningless but rhythmic words when they like the sounds; their nursery rhymes and games are often based on repeated sounds. Music creates various moods: a band marches to a crisp beat; a military funeral is paced by a slow, muffled drum; a wedding march is stately, loud, and joyful. At a football game excitement is stirred up by the rhythmic cheers. Many advertisers depend on slogans repeating vowel and consonant sounds. We respond emotionally to recurring accents and sounds.

In making his lines agreeable, the poet is limited only by what the human voice can say and what the human ear can hear. He arranges his syllables into patterns: stress (the accent put on syllables), sound sequences (one sound echoing another), pitch (the rise and fall of the voice), pause (the points where silence is indicated by the syntax), and tempo (the time it takes to speak the sound).

METER

A single rhythmic line of poetry is called a *verse*, and is described according to its *meter*, the pattern of repetition built into the verse by the organized rhythmic sounds of speech. The meter is based on the fact that the syllables of English words are either stressed or unstressed. As we say a word, we put more emphasis on one syllable than on another, and each of the syllables is spoken with a certain pitch (high or low on the musical scale), with varying loudness, and with a particular length (the time it takes to say it).

If, for example, we read in a dictionary the entry de•light′, the separation of the word indicates that the word has two syllables, and the accent mark (′) shows that we stress the second syllable in speaking. In marking the stress in poetry, we put the accent mark over the syllable.

Words of one syllable are not marked with an accent in the dictionary, because whether they are accented or not depends on their use in a sentence. For example, a word like *track*, unaccented in "deer track," is accented in "the track of a deer."

So as the poet arranges the stresses (the meter) in a verse, he uses the normal pronunciations of words, and single syllable words will be accented according to their meaning. The accent can fall on the odd-numbered syllables, on the even-numbered syllables, or on every third syllable, with each pattern creating a distinctive rhythm, or repetition, of accented beats. Variations most often throw the accent heavily on one or more successively stressed syllables.

Whatever rhythm the poet sets up at the beginning will be maintained throughout his lines, unless he works in variations. The variations are used to break the monotony of continuous lines or, more importantly, to emphasize key words or ideas in the meaning.

The reader's marking of the beats in a line of poetry is called *scanning*. We scan not only to know the meter and to give it a name, but to find the relation of the sound pattern to the meaning of the poem. To scan, we first count the number of syllables in each line:

1 2 3 4 5 6 7 8
Had we but world e nough, and time,

1 2 3 4 5 6 7 8
This coy ness, La dy, were no crime.

Since some syllables receive a heavier stress than others, we then mark off those heavier stresses with the symbol ′, and the minor ones with the symbol ⌣. If you are in doubt about where a word is stressed or where syllables end, use a dictionary.

Hăd wé | bŭt wórld | ĕ nóugh, | ănd tíme, |

Thĭs cóy | nĕss, Lá | dy̆, wére | nŏ críme. |

The pattern repeated in the above line of poetry is unstressed and stressed, repeated four times in each verse. Each of those four repeated patterns is known as a *foot*, and each foot is marked off with vertical lines. The sounds of the verses can thus be represented by visual symbols.

Except in irregular lines, we should be able to work out the meter from any word of more than one syllable. We said earlier that monosyllables may be stressed or not, depending on the normal rhythm and meaning involved in speaking the line. In a word like *flowers* in the following line, we know that the accent falls on the first syllable. If we work forward and backward from that fact, we get

Whĕn spríng, | wĭth déw | y̆ flów | ĕrs cóld, |

Our decision on what makes a foot comes from a knowledge of the various kinds of feet that are most often used in English poetry. There are four major types of feet.

1. The most common foot in English is the *iamb*, a weak syllable followed by a strong one: dĕ líght. An iambic line: Cŏme líve | wĭth mé | ănd bé | my̆ lóve, |

2. The *trochee* is a strong syllable followed by a weak one: héav ĕn. A trochaic line: Thén thĕ | lít tlĕ | Hí ă | wáth ă |

3. The *dactyl* is a strong, weak, weak beat: fool ish ly. A dactylic line: This is the | for est pri | me val. | This line, used by Longfellow, drops the final syllable, but is predominantly dactylic.

4. The *anapest* is a weak, weak, strong beat: in ter rupt. An anapestic line: O well | for the fish | er man's boy. | The first foot here is iambic; thereafter the feet are anapestic. We name a verse according to the predominant meter.

A common type of variation in these meters is the *spondee,* two successive accented syllables used as a substitution for a single foot in any other metrical pattern.

A further refinement in talking about poetry comes in describing the verse by the number of feet. Since each foot has only one strong accent, we can determine the number of feet in a line by the number of stressed, or strong, accents. In the last line of poetry marked off above, there are three feet. We describe the line, or verse, by saying that it is an anapestic trimeter, or a three-stress anapestic line.

The classical way of referring to the number of feet is through the use of Greek prefixes: a line of one foot, monometer; two feet, dimeter; three feet, trimeter; four feet, tetrameter; five feet, pentameter; six feet, hexameter, etc. Nowadays, however, it is more common to refer to a four-stress or five-stress line, using English terminology.

FREE VERSE

Some poets have preferred to write with more freedom than that offered by regular metrical patterns. They chose free verse, which lacks regular meter and rhyme and varies in length of line. It is based on the rhythm of the spoken language and makes use of repeated words or parallel grammatical structures (phrases, clauses, or sentences, for instance). As an example, read the first stanza of Whitman's "Pioneers! O Pioneers!"

Come my tan-faced children,
Follow well in order, get your weapons ready,
Have you your pistols? have you your sharp-edged axes?
Pioneers! O pioneers!

Notice the parallel structure in the use of repeated imperative verbs—"Come," "Follow," "Get"—and the repeated rhythm in each demand. The two questions in the third line each repeat a similar grammatical structure. The stanza ends with the repetition of the word "pioneers." In such ways the writer gives a sense of rhythm to the lines without using regular meter or rhyme. See also the use of free verse in "Lunch on Omaha Beach."

BLANK VERSE

Some of the greatest poetry in English, especially that of Shakespeare and Milton, is written for the most part in blank verse, unrhymed iambic pentameter. Here are two examples:

Their glory withered: as, when Heaven's fire
Has scathed the forest oaks or mountain pines.
Milton, "Paradise Lost"

It may be that the gulfs will wash us down;
It may be we shall touch the Happy Isles,
And see the great Achilles, whom we knew.
Tennyson, "Ulysses"

PAUSE

Another part of metrics is the marking of any strong pause (a silence) in the rhythm of a verse. The device used for marking a pause is a *caesura* (||). The silence is forced on us by the natural pause that we make in speaking a sentence. Minor pauses always follow syntactical units: phrases, clauses, sentences. The number of such pauses has much to do with the tempo with which we read a line. The caesura marks only major pauses, usually one to a line, most often near the middle of a line.

In the following lines by Shakespeare, the caesura rises from the syntax:

Full fathom five || thy father lies;
Of his bones || are coral made.

Another example is

Come live with me || and be my love

Sometimes the caesura is forced on us by the punctuation:

Had we but world enough, || and time
This coyness, || Lady, || were no crime.

Or Sassoon's,

I'd toddle safely home and die— || in bed.

An example of caesuras rising from both punctuation and syntax can be seen in the following stanza from Alfred Noyes's "A Song of Sherwood."

Sherwood in the twilight, || is Robin Hood awake?
Gray and ghostly shadows || are gliding through the brake,
Shadows of the dappled deer, || dreaming of the morn,
Dreaming of a shadowy man || that winds a shadowy horn.

A caesura is a breath pause, which helps the poet imitate the patterns of ordinary speech. It usually falls near the middle of a line, but for variety it is sometimes placed near the beginning or end of the line. When Sassoon, in the line above, puts his pause before "in bed," he throws weight on the irony of the situation described in "Base Details."

In reading poetry aloud, pause slightly at the end of a run-on line (one in which the sense goes on to the next line). The pitch of the voice should stay up at such points, as it does at a caesura. The exception is when the sentence ends with the verse or caesura; then the voice does drop.

One further consideration in dealing with meter is that a poet will sometimes use words in which two syllables will be spoken quickly to form one beat in an otherwise regular line. For example, in Milton's line "Of man's first disobedience, and the fruit," the word is pronounced disobed-yence. Thus the verse keeps to a ten-syllable-sounding line. Some poets will write *never* as ne'er to get a similar effect. The device is known as *syncope*, the dropping of an unstressed vowel or the omission of a consonant.

VARIATION

In spite of the fact that we have been suggesting a kind of regularity in poetry, it does not exist so neatly in practice. If it did, the resultant poem would have a monotonous sound.

> O Captain! my Captain! our fearful trip is done,
> The ship has weathered every rack, the prize we sought is
>   won,
> The port is near, the bells I hear, the people all exulting,
> While follow eyes the steady keel, the vessel grim and
>   daring.
>
> Whitman, "O Captain! My Captain"

Regularity can turn poetry into a jingle.

What most often happens is that a poem begins with a few lines of regular rhythm and then makes a substitution. At that point, a line which contains primarily a series of one type of foot may include a foot of another type. Yeats's line "Ăll oth | ĕr lov | ĕrs be | ĭng ĕs tranged | ŏr dead" contains two variations. The first three feet and the fifth are iambic, but the fourth is anapestic. The final syllable of "estranged" is slurred over and pronounced as part of the heavily accented previous syllable (syncope).

Such a change in beat throws emphasis on the point where change takes place. If the line had been written in regular meter (Ăll oth | ĕr lov | ĕrs are | ă part | ŏr dead) we would not have the emphasis that comes on "estranged" when our expectation of regularity is changed. As Yeats goes back to an iambic foot, the beat hits harder on "dead" than it would have if the line were regular.

Though we may mark off the various stresses, as we did in the line by Yeats, we must assume that the syntax of the sentence causes us to read with more emphasis on some sounds. The first syllable of "other" must be quickly complemented by the second syllable, but the word "dead" completes a unit of thought and naturally receives more emphasis.

Earlier we discussed the diction of a few lines of Eberhart's "To a Groundhog." Now listen to the sound:

> In June, | a mid | the gold | en field |
> I saw | a ground | hog ly | ing dead. |
> Dead | lay he; | my sens | es shook, |
> And mind | out shot | our na | ked frailty. |

The substitution comes in line three. The first accent falls hard on "dead," a word that emphasizes what the lines are about. "Frailty" is marked as one syllable because it has to be slurred (syncope).

In the earlier discussion of Blake's "The Sick Rose," we found that critics do not agree on its meaning. Yet when we scan the lines, we find the greatest point of emphasis in the next to the last line, "And his dark | secret | love. The heavy accents falling together on "dark" and "secret" and "love," may indicate that the poem is about illicit love.

Sassoon's "Base Details" begins with four lines of iambic pentameter, and then shifts to "Guzzling and gulping in the best hotel." By throwing the accent on the first syllable of guzzling, Sassoon emphasizes the behavior of the majors.

In "Lunch on Omaha Beach," when Noll wants to emphasize the killing that took place in the war, he writes, "Death's great bronze mares," with four successive heavy stresses.

SOUND SEQUENCE

The echoing of sound that makes up much of the music of poetry is based on the repetition of the sounds of vowels and consonants. The most common repetitions of sounds in related words are known as *alliteration*, *assonance*, and *rhyme*. All tend to bind words together in meaning as well as in sound.

Alliteration is the repetition of identical initial consonant or vowel sounds in words placed closely together. Sassoon, for example, uses "puffy petulant," "guzzling and gulping," "reading the roll." Though the letters are different, the initial sounds of "close" and "quench" are the same in Seeger's "And close my eyes and quench my breath."

In "A Song of Sherwood," quoted earlier, notice the *g* and *d* sounds:

> Gray and ghostly shadows are gliding through the brake,
> Shadows of the dappled deer, dreaming of the morn.

And in H. D.'s lines, the *th* and *p* sounds:

> Fruit that cannot drop
> through this thick air—
> fruit cannot fall into heat
> that presses up and blunts
> the points of pears
> and rounds the grapes.

The sound of a line should have some connection with the sense. In Coleridge's lines describing the sailing of a ship, an *f* sound is repeated;

> The fair breeze blew, the white foam flew,
> The furrow followed free.

Coleridge is describing a ship sailing under a strong breeze. The letter *f*, heavily accented, is connected to the sound of wind; it is an aspirated sound, one made with a puff of breath.

An interpretation of the connection between sound and sense can be made only if the sound does fit the meaning; the sounds themselves cannot create meaning. If Coleridge had written "The fleet floated free on a flat sea," we could not argue that the *f* sound represented puffs of wind. The sound can support the sense.

"The murmuring of innumerable bees" has often been cited as imitating the hum of bees; but, as John Crowe Ransom has pointed out, "The murdering of innumerable beeves" sounds the same. Sound cannot be considered separate from meaning; but if the sound does reflect the meaning, we should notice it.

Assonance, another type of sound echoing, is the repetition of vowel sounds. The example cited earlier from Coleridge also repeats an *o* sound three times in "the furrow followed free." Another example is the repetition of the *i* and *a* sounds (the sounds, as opposed to the printed letter) in the line "In Xanadu did Kubla Kahn," (the first *a* does not sound the same as the others and is not an example of assonance), or the *o*-sound in Waller's "Go, lovely Rose."

If the words, usually at the ends of lines, end with identical or similar sounds, we consider that they rhyme. The rhyme depends on the similarity in the sound of the vowel and the following consonants, but the previous consonant sounds may be different—as in *tan* and *man*. Normal rhyme repeats the sound exactly—*spring* and *wing*; imperfect rhyme, used deliberately to break the monotony of exact rhyme, makes slight changes in the vowel sounds—*love* and *prove*.

When rhyme is used, it has several functions. It is pleasant to the ear and also marks the end of a verse. In addition, it organizes the pattern of a stanza or poem. Most importantly, it has meaning in that certain words are brought together by rhyme; they may bind ideas together or contrast them.

The pattern of rhymes is referred to as the *rhyme scheme*. When the first line ends, we can symbolize the sound of a rhyming word with the letter *a*. When we come to a similar rhyme, we mark that, too, with an *a*. When a second and different rhyme is used, we call it *b*, and its rhyming partner is also *b*. A different set of rhymes will be marked with *c*'s, and so on.

In an ode on Cromwell, Marvell uses a four-line stanza with the simple rhyme scheme *a a b b*; that is, the first two lines rhyme, as do the third and fourth.

Then burning through the air he went,
And palaces and temples rent;
  And Caesar's head at last
  Did through his laurels blast.

The unit for marking the rhyme scheme of a long poem divided into stanzas is each stanza alone. Marvell goes on using different rhymes, but the *a a b b* pattern continues:

'Tis madness to resist or blame
The face of angry heaven's flame;
  And if we would speak true,
  Much to the man is due.

Some of the meaning of a stanza can be carried by its rhyme. Notice in the first stanza of Marvell's ode that the rhyming of "at last" with a strong word like "blast" comes as a surprise and also fits the meaning. Cromwell had seemed to be a savior, but became a Caesar, a dictator, an idea that blasts forth. The rhyme fits the meaning.

THE ORGANIZATION OF THE POEM

A poem may be organized into several basic patterns: into stanzas; into continuous form, with one line after another; or into traditional forms like the sonnet or ballad.

The *stanza* (a rough equivalent of a prose paragraph) is a common pattern. A certain number of lines establishes a form for the stanza that is repeated ordinarily through the poem, usually with the same rhyme scheme. Since the variety in stanza forms is great, we can only say that you should look at the rhyme scheme, notice whether and how the meaning is related to other stanzas, and determine what grammatical units are included.

Another common organization for a poem is a *sonnet*, a poem of fourteen lines. Historically there are two major forms of the sonnet: the Petrarchan or Italian, and the Shakespearean. The Petrarchan rhymes *a b b a a b b a c d c d c d*; it falls into two parts: an octet (eight lines) made up of two quatrains (four-line sections) and a sestet (a unit of six lines). John Keats's "On First Looking into Chapman's Homer" is a good example.

Much have I travelled in the realms of gold,
And many goodly states and kingdoms seen;
Round many western islands have I been
Which bards in fealty to Apollo hold.
Oft of one wide expanse had I been told
That deep-browed Homer ruled as his demesne;
Yet did I never breathe its pure serene
Till I heard Chapman speak out loud and bold:
Then felt I like some watcher of the skies
When a new planet swims into his ken;
Or like stout Cortez when with eagle eyes
He stared at the Pacific—and all his men
Looked at each other with a wild surmise—
Silent, upon a peak in Darien.

In the first four lines, the poet metaphorically describes his reading in ancient literature (in translations). In the second quatrain, he speaks of knowing the work of Homer (probably in Pope's stilted translation), but he never realized how great Homer was until he read Chapman's translation. Then the turn into the sestet gives the effect of his reading Chapman, comparing the experience first with an astronomer's seeing a new planet and then with Cortez's discovering the Pacific Ocean (of course Balboa discovered the Pacific, but the error hardly matters here, since both men were explorers). The caesura in the last line falls after "silent," emphasizing how difficult it is to express the feeling that followed the discovery of Chapman's work. You will also notice a shift in the diction. In the first eight lines while Keats is speaking of other translations, his choice of words is also a bit stilted. When he shifts in the sestet to Chapman's "loud and bold" diction, Keats himself changes his manner of speaking.

The Shakespearean sonnet rhymes *a b a b c d c d e f e f g g*. Each quatrain usually contains a major image, and the final couplet is a general summary of the meaning of the sonnet. Here is Shakespeare's Sonnet 18:

Shall I compare thee to a summer's day?
Thou art more lovely and more temperate:
Rough winds do shake the darling buds of May,
And summer's lease hath all too short a date:
Sometime too hot the eye of heaven shines,

And often is his gold complexion dimm'd;
And every fair from fair sometimes declines,
By chance or nature's changing course untrimm'd:
But thy eternal summer shall not fade,
Nor lose possession of that fair thou owest;
Nor shall death brag thou wanderest in his shade,
When in eternal lines to time thou growest:
So long as men can breathe, or eyes can see,
So long lives this, and this gives life to thee.

This Shakespearean sonnet contains fourteen lines on a single idea or emotion. It consists of three quatrains (a four-verse grouping of lines) and a concluding couplet. The rhyme scheme binds together each of three sets of four lines and the concluding couplet.

Shakespeare begins the sonnet by asking a question of his loved one and then gives an answer. Even a summer's day may be disturbed by "rough winds," and summer is too brief. There is the implied question, Shall I compare you to the sun? Again the answer is no. The sun ("the eye of heaven") may grow too strong, or be "dimm'd" by clouds; everything beautiful in nature changes. In the third quatrain the poet promises that his love's beauty ("eternal summer") shall not fade and that she shall not lose what she owns ("owest"); nor shall death overcome that beauty. Then comes the final promise in the couplet: as long as men live, so long will this poem live, and it will hold your beauty in memory. You can see that the structure of a sonnet is closely related to the meaning being expressed.

One other commonly used stanza is that of the ballad, a four-line stanza, with alternating lines of iambic tetrameter (four stresses) and iambic trimeter (three stresses), and with the second and fourth lines rhyming.

There lived a wife at Usher's Well,
  And a wealthy wife was she;
She had three stout and stalwart sons,
  And sent them o'er the sea.

TEMPO

The musical effect of a line is also determined by its tempo, the time it takes to read it. It is determined by close attention to the vowel and consonant sounds. The long vowels take longer to say and are louder than short vowels. A line containing liquid consonants—*l, m, n, w, v*—will flow swiftly. A cluster of hard consonants—*d, t, g, k*—will slow a line. The device of using a series of sounds that are pleasant to the ear is known as *euphony*. Harshness, created by grouping sounds that are difficult to speak, is known as *cacophony*.

A poet will suit all these devices to the purpose demanded by the relationship of sound and sense. Lanier, in "Song of the Chattahoochee," is describing the movement of a river and trying to match the tempo of the lines to that movement.

> Out of the hills of Habersham,
> Down the valleys of Hall,
> I hurry amain to reach the plain,
> Run the rapid and leap the fall,
> Split at the rock and together again,
> Accept my bed, or narrow or wide,
> And flee from folly on every side
> With a lover's pain to attain the plain
> Far from the hills of Habersham,
> Far from the valleys of Hall.

The short vowels, one-syllable words, and liquid sounds make the reader pound along like a brook moving downhill. But when the water reaches the meadow and slows up in the second stanza, the harsher consonants, *d*'s and *t*'s, and the long vowels compel the reader to slow down.

> All down the hills of Habersham,
> All through the valleys of Hall,
> The rushes cried *Abide, abide,*
> The willful waterweeds held me thrall,
> The laving laurel turned my tide,
> The ferns and the fondling grass said *Stay,*
> The dewberry dipped for to work delay,
> And the little reeds sighed *Abide, abide,*
> *Here in the hills of Habersham,*
> *Here in the valleys of Hall.*

EXERCISES

1. Write an essay in which you discuss in detail Lanier's use of sound in any two consecutive lines of the first stanza and any two consecutive lines in the second stanza. Describe his use of alliteration, assonance, meter, and tempo in the lines you choose. Begin by copying the following paragraph:

> Lanier in "Song of the Chattahoochee" is describing the movement of a river, and the sound of the poem reflects the meaning as the motion turns from fast to slow. To accomplish this change, he makes use of appropriate alliteration, assonance, meter, and tempo.

Then go on to discuss in the next paragraph the lines you choose in stanza one; be sure to quote the lines. After pointing out the ways in which Lanier uses the techniques mentioned in the opening paragraph, go on to discuss the second pair of lines.

2. In the following excerpt from Pope's "An Essay on Criticism," the poet is arguing that the sound of a poem should fit its meaning. Write an essay in which you analyze in detail at least four lines of the poem. Show the connection between the sound of each line and the meaning of the line. Be specific about the devices by which the author gets his effect.

> True ease in writing comes from art, not chance,
> As those move easiest who have learned to dance.
> 'Tis not enough no harshness gives offense,
> The sound must seem an echo to the sense:
> Soft is the strain when Zephyr gently blows,
> And the smooth stream in smoother numbers flows:
> But when loud surges lash the sounding shore,
> The hoarse, rough verse should like the torrent roar:
> When Ajax strives some rock's vast weight to throw,
> The line too labors, and the words move slow;
> Not so, when swift Camilla scours the plain,
> Flies o'er th' unbending corn, and skims along the main.
> Hear how Timotheus' varied lays surprise,
> And bid alternate passions fall and rise!

Before you write, copy the lines that you intend to deal with. Mark off the meter of each line. Underline the various devices of alliteration, assonance, euphony, cacophony, and tempo that you will use to prove your points.

After you write your opening paragraph indicating what your paper is about and summarizing what you intend to say, help your reader by including in each paragraph the quoted line that you are discussing. State its meaning and then show how the writer has connected the sound of the line to that meaning.

The argument here is that the sound of a poem is integrally linked to its meaning. If one were to read the following poem according to its meter alone, it would fall into a pattern of sing-song. Try reading it that way.

THE MAN HE KILLED — **Thomas Hardy**

"Had he and I but met
By some old ancient inn,
We should have sat us down to wet
Right many a nipperkin!

"But ranged as infantry,
And staring face to face,
I shot at him as he at me,
And killed him in his place.

"I shot him dead because—
Because he was my foe,
Just so: my foe of course he was;
That's clear enough; although

"He thought he'd 'list, perhaps,
Off-hand-like—just as I—
Was out of work—had sold his traps—
No other reason why.

"Yes; quaint and curious war is!
You shoot a fellow down
You'd treat, if met where any bar is,
Or help to half-a-crown."

Now consider the meaning by mentally underlining the key words in the sense of the poem (words like "met," "inn," "sat us down," "nipperkin," "ranged," "infantry"). Then if you accent those words more than others, you do not ignore the meter, but rather set up a tension between the meaning and the rhythm that gives a more satisfactory reading. Read the poem again, paying more attention to the key words in the meaning.

3. Write an essay on the use of pauses in "The Man He Killed." Before you write, consider the following questions: What is the main idea? What do you learn about the speaker in the poem? How does Hardy inject pauses in stanzas 3 and 4? How do the pauses relate to the meaning of the poem?

Begin your essay by completing the following statement: In "The Man He Killed" Hardy is arguing that . . . Go on to answer the first two questions. In your second paragraph answer the third question. Then go on in your other paragraphs to answer the fourth and fifth questions. Make sure that your individual paragraphs let the reader know what you are talking about. You can do this by restating the questions in the form of statements.

Questions on Poetry

What is the occasion of the poem? What situation is being described? Who is the speaker? Is the speaker taking part in the action? Are other voices speaking? Is there an implied audience for the poem?

What attitude is the speaker taking toward his subject? Is he serious, amused, angry, humorous, or what? Is the diction concrete or abstract? What are the connotations of the key words and images? Does the context give unusual meanings to words? Are common words used in uncommon ways? Does the tone of the poem indicate that the words are used ironically? Are there examples of poetic amiguity?

How is the poem organized? Are key words repeated? What connections do you see between the images? How are the sentences and stanzas linked? How is the grammar related to the meaning? Is there a logical progression of ideas? Is use made of connections of time, space, comparison, contrast, cause and effect? Why is the poem organized as it is? Is the pattern of organization related to the meaning?

Do the images have a literal or metaphoric meaning? If the passage is metaphoric, what two things are being compared? Which is the literal term and which is the figurative? In what ways are the two things alike? What do the figurative phrases mean literally? Is there any use of symbols? What do they stand for?

What is the connection between sound and meaning? What use has the poet made of alliteration and assonance? What is the predominant meter of the poem? Where there are exceptions to the regular beat, what changes are made in the emphasis? Does the variation affect the meaning? What use is made of pause? In what tempo should the various lines be read? Does the meaning help in determining the tempo? How does the writer manage to vary the tempo?

What is the significance of the title? Does it have more than one meaning? What is the theme of the poem?

3

DRAMA

READING PLAYS

Drama employs many techniques common to other genres of fiction, but it also necessitates important differences, which can be understood by examining the possibilities and limitations that exist for a writer of novels or short stories and a writer of drama. Though each tells a story, he does so in a different way.

The narrative fiction writer may use dramatic techniques, but he is telling a story that each of us will sit and read alone. As we saw earlier, he sets up a voice to speak for him, a narrator who may take part in the action, or who may stand outside the story yet know all that needs to be known. The narrative writer can tell us what people look like, what they think, what tones they speak in, and what they are doing. He can describe places and take us quickly to another scene. By manipulating the time scheme, he can let us know what is happening in two different places at the same time. After beginning at one point in time, he can manipulate a flashback to a previous time. Above all, he can focus our attention on one person or one thing. He can easily move his focus to point out actions or things that some characters may overlook, or he can move in for closeups and let us, for example, read a letter in someone's hand. The storyteller can stop at any time to summarize the action.

A playwright has fewer options. He puts down words that actors will interpret, as a composer writes the notes that a violinist will play. In a play, all the action must be shown. The usual method is to create a setting of a three-sided room, with the fourth wall open to the audience; or the scene may be set out of doors. These obvious and simple facts have a great effect on what the playwright can and cannot do. The author remains outside the action of the play. Characterization in the play is accomplished by speech and by whatever actions add to the interpretation. (Since the means of characterization are somewhat limited, the writer often sets up a contrasting character to bring out the qualities of the major character.) The tone of a line will be part of its meaning. The tempo of a scene will be determined partly by the length of speeches and by implied pauses. No words can be wasted; each speech must move the play along lines suggested by the central theme. What a person is thinking can be suggested by the way he says a line and what he does as he says it. The mood can also be affected by stage lighting.

A playwright must compress his action; even a three or five act play will take little longer than two hours. Exposition must be succinct, and characterization drawn in broad strokes. What may seem to be a trivial action must have importance in the meaning of the whole. Repeated phrases, metaphors, or symbols must be obvious and connected to the meaning of the play.

The action must be unified in terms of time and space. The stage itself is limited to at most two or three changes of setting, and often there will be only a single setting. What happens offstage is described by one of the actors. The time span must be limited. The play begins in the middle of a situation, as close to the end as possible. The "end" means the final action; "as possible" means only that the motivation is supplied for the big climactic scene, the dénouement, the point at which we can see how things will turn out.

The writer must also keep the audience's attention where he wants it. Small objects are not seen unless they are pointed at. Letters must be read aloud. If a character is to be stabbed with a letter opener, someone must pick it up early in the play and comment on how dangerous it is; after the crime, someone must say that the weapon is the same one shown earlier.

The fact of an audience makes a play a group experience. The action cannot be as subtle as that in fiction. Lines must carry meaning when they are first heard. A funny line may seem funnier because a group is reacting to it, and the individual is reacting to the group. Watching something happen also makes the play seem real, because actors are living out their fate on the stage before us. Though we are only watching, we cannot help but participate by identifying with someone who represents our own fears, hopes, or beliefs.

The actor must fit the part he plays. When he comes onstage, we must figure out who he is, why he is here, what his relationship is to the other characters, where the action is taking place, and what problem is about to be faced. The writer must offer this information in his exposition, and it must be worked naturally into the dialogue of the play. Often this information may be presented several times, from different characters with different points of view. One reason for this is that a playwright, writing for an audience and depending on the spoken word, must repeat important ideas. Shakespeare commonly tells his audience what is going to happen, has it happen, and then tells the audience that it has happened. For example, Hamlet tells Horatio (and, of course, the audience) to watch the King's reaction to the "play within the play," the King reacts, and Hamlet and Horatio discuss his reaction. Shakespeare then knew that even the dullest mind would get his point.

In the act of sitting and reading a play, we must put ourselves imaginatively into directing the play, into creating a performance. We must imagine what type of person should play each part, what the tone and tempo of each spoken line should be, where the pauses should occur, what action should accompany each speech, and in what kind of setting the play should be performed.

A playwright will sometimes give us some obvious aids. His stage directions may describe the setting, or it may be described by a character. He may on occasion put a word in parenthesis to describe the tone—(menacingly). Or he may use the same device to show what a person should be doing—(looking wildly around the room)—or to announce entrances and exits—(John enters). In such ways the playwright can extend his medium.

The playwright can also experiment with techniques more common to narrative fiction. In *Our Town*, Thornton Wilder uses the character of a stage manager, who talks directly to the audience, explains what is going on, speaks directly to the characters, and withdraws to watch the action, to help convey the author's meaning and "cue" the audience's responses. This device is not new; it adapts the device of the Greek chorus. Wilder merely substituted one man for the chorus. Eugene O'Neill uses the mannerism of having characters speak to one another and then turn to the audience to say what they are thinking, which is an exaggeration of Shakespearean soliloquies. The assumption is that the other characters do not hear these speeches. Many writers use "asides" in which the actor speaks briefly to the audience—for example, "He doesn't know who I am"—and then turns back to his dialogue. In Arthur Miller's *Death of a Salesman*, much of the action is taken up with moments in which Willy Loman's mind retreats into recollections of the past, which are then acted out on the stage. At such moments a gauze curtain falls, blocking out the apartment houses in the background and giving the impression of trees in their stead.

Techniques like these may make our reading of plays easier, helping us to understand and to see imaginatively. But the most important act of reading is "hearing" the lines as we read. The way a line is said is what gives it meaning in a play. Much of the criticism about how the part of Shakespeare's Hamlet should be played, for example, is really an argument about how the lines should be spoken by the actor. Our interpretation of the following play, "The Stronger," will be determined by how we think Mrs. X will speak certain key lines. Working out the tones of the lines in a play is an imaginative act. The ability to do it well, to give meaning to the lines, is what makes great actors and actresses.

"The Stronger," by the Swedish playwright August Strindberg, was first produced in 1889. It is a brief monologue, interrupted at various times only by the actions of a second character. The play demonstrates how much can be learned by listening to a person talk. If we pay careful attention and "hear" the lines, we can learn much of the past of three characters and their various relationships.

Because the play is so carefully written and so economically constructed, you will need to read it more than once. You must work out imaginatively the various tones of voice used by the actress who speaks the lines, and notice especially where one tone ends and another takes over, and why. You must "see" the actresses move and determine what those motions add to the meaning of the words. Read as though you yourself were about to play the part, as though you had to give meaning to the words.

THE STRONGER

August Strindberg

Characters

MRS. X., an actress, married
MISS Y., an actress, unmarried
A WAITRESS

SCENE. *The corner of a ladies' cafe. Two little iron tables, a red velvet sofa, several chairs. Enter MRS. X., dressed in winter clothes, carrying a Japanese basket on her arm.*

MISS Y: sits with a half-empty beer bottle before her, reading an illustrated paper, which she changes later for another.

MRS. X: Good afternoon, Amelia. Your'e sitting here alone on Christmas eve like a poor bachelor!

MISS Y: (*Looks up, nods, and resumes her reading.*)

MRS. X: Do you know it really hurts me to see you like this, alone, in a café, and on Christmas eve, too. It makes me feel as I did one time when I saw a bridal party in a Paris restaurant, and the bride sat reading a comic paper, while the groom played billiards with the witnesses. Huh, thought I, with such a beginning, what will follow, and what will be the end? He played billiards on his wedding eve! (*MISS Y. starts to speak*) And she read a comic paper, you mean? Well, they are not altogether the same thing.

(*A WAITRESS enters, places a cup of chocolate before MRS. X. and goes out.*)

MRS. X: You know what, Amelia! I believe you would have done better to have kept him! Do you remember, I was the first to say "Forgive him?" Do you remember that? You would be married now and have a home. Remember that Christmas when you went out to visit your fiancé's parents in the country? How you gloried in the happiness of home life and really longed to quit the theatre forever? Yes, Amelia dear, home is the best of all —next to the theatre—and as for children—well, you don't understand that.

MISS Y: (*Looks up scornfully.*)

(*MRS. X. sips a few spoonfuls out of the cup, then opens her basket and shows Christmas presents.*)

MRS. X: Now you shall see what I bought for my piggywigs. [*Takes up a doll*] Look at this! This is for Lisa, ha! Do you see how she can roll her eyes and turn her head, eh? And here is Maja's popgun.

(*Loads it and shoots at MISS Y.*)

MISS Y: (*Makes a startled gesture.*)

MRS. X: Did I frighten you? Do you think I would like to shoot you, eh? On my soul, if I don't think you did! If you wanted to shoot *me* it wouldn't be so surprising, because I stood in your way—and I know you can never forget that—although I was absolutely innocent. You still believe I intrigued and got you out of the Stora theatre, but I didn't. I didn't do that, although you think so. Well, it doesn't make any difference what I say to you. You still believe I did it. (*Takes up a pair of embroidered slippers*) And these are for my better half. I embroidered them myself—I can't bear tulips, but he wants tulips on everything.

MISS Y: (*Looks up ironically and curiously.*)

MRS. X: (*putting a hand in each slipper*) See what little feet Bob has! What? And you should see what a splendid stride he has! You've never seen him in slippers! (*MISS Y. laughs aloud.*) Look! (*She makes the slippers walk on the table. MISS Y. laughs loudly.*) And when he is grumpy he stamps like this with his foot. "What! damn those servants who can never learn to make coffee. Oh, now those creatures haven't trimmed the lamp wick properly!" And then there are draughts on the floor and his feet are cold. "Ugh, how cold it is; the stupid idiots can never keep the fire going." (*She rubs the slippers together, one sole over the other.*)

MISS Y: (*Shrieks with laughter.*)

MRS. X: And then he comes home and has to hunt for his slippers which Marie has stuck under the chiffonier—oh, but it's sinful to sit here and make fun of one's husband this way when he is kind and a good little man. You ought to have had such a husband, Amelia. What are you laughing at? What? What? And you see he's true to me. Yes, I'm sure of that, because he told me himself—what are you laughing at?—that when I was touring in Norway that brazen Frederika came and wanted to seduce him! Can you fancy anything so infamous? (*pause*) I'd have torn her eyes out if she had come to see him when I was at home. (*pause*) It was lucky that Bob told me about it himself and that it didn't reach me through gossip. (*pause*) But would you believe it, Frederika wasn't the only one! I don't know why, but the women are crazy about my husband. They must think he has influence about getting them theatrical engagements, because he is connected with the government. Perhaps you were after him yourself. I didn't use to trust you any too much. But now I know he never bothered his head about you, and you always seemed to have a grudge against him someway.

(*Pause. They look at each other in a puzzled way.*)

MRS. X: Come and see us this evening, Amelia, and show us that you're not put out with us—not put out with me at any rate. I don't know, but I think it would be uncomfortable to have you for an enemy. Perhaps it's because I stood in your way (*more slowly*) or—I really—don't know why—in particular.

(*Pause. MISS Y. stares at MRS. X. curiously.*)

MRS. X: (*thoughtfully*) Our acquaintance has been so queer. When I saw you for the first time I was afraid of you, so afraid that I didn't dare let you out of my sight; no matter when or where, I always found myself near you —I didn't dare have you for an enemy, so I became your friend. But there was always discord when you came to our house, because I saw that my husband couldn't endure you, and the whole thing seemed as awry to me as an ill-fitting gown—and I did all I could to make him friendly toward you, but with no success until you became engaged. Then came a violent friendship between you, so that it looked all at once as though you both dared show your real feelings only when you were secure—and then—how was it later? I didn't get jealous—strange to say! And I remember at the christening, when you acted as godmother, I made him kiss you—he did so, and you became so confused—as it were; I didn't notice it then—didn't think about it later, either—have never thought about it until—now! (*Rises suddenly.*) Why are you silent? You haven't said a word this whole time, but you have let me go on talking! You have sat there, and your eyes have reeled out of me all these thoughts which lay like raw silk in its cocoon—thoughts—suspicious thoughts, perhaps. Let me see—why did you break your engagement? Why do you never come to our house any more? Why won't you come to see us tonight?

(*MISS Y. appears as if about to speak.*)

MRS. X: Hush, you needn't speak—I understand it all! It was because—and because—and because! Yes, yes! Now all the accounts balance. That's it. Fie, I won't sit at the same table with you. (*Moves her things to another table.*) That's the reason I had to embroider tulips—which I hate—on his slippers, because you are fond of tulips; that's why (*throws slippers on the floor*) we go to Lake Mälarn in the summer, because you don't like salt water; that's why my boy is named Eskil—because it's your father's name; that's why I wear your colors, read your authors, eat your favorite dishes, drink your drinks—chocolate, for instance; that's why—oh—my God—it's terrible, when I think about it, it's terrible. Everything, everything came from you to me, even your passions. Your soul crept into mine, like a worm into an apple, ate and ate, bored and bored, until nothing was left but the rind and a little black dust within. I wanted to get away from you, but I couldn't; you lay like a snake and charmed me with your black eyes; I felt that when I lifted my wings they only dragged me down; I lay in the water with bound feet, and the stronger I strove to keep up the deeper I worked myself down, down, until I sank to the bottom, where you lay like a giant crab to clutch me in your claws—and there I am lying now.

I hate you, hate you, hate you! And you only sit there silent—silent and indifferent; indifferent whether it's new moon or waning moon, Christmas or New Year's, whether others are happy or unhappy; without power to hate or to love; as quiet as a stork by a rat hole—you couldn't scent your prey and capture it, but you could lie in wait for it! You sit here in your corner of the café—did you know it's called "The Rat Trap" for you?—and read the papers to see if misfortune hasn't befallen someone, to see if someone hasn't been given notice at the theatre, perhaps; you sit here and calculate about your next victim and reckon on your chances of recompense like a pilot in a shipwreck. Poor Amelia, I pity you, nevertheless, because I know you are unhappy, unhappy like one who has been wounded, and angry because you are wounded. I can't be angry with you, no matter how much I want to be—because you come out the weaker one. Yes, all that with Bob doesn't trouble me. What is that to me, after all? And what difference does it make whether I learned to drink chocolate from you or some one else. (*Sips a spoonful from her cup*) Besides, chocolate is very healthful. And if you taught me how to dress—tant mieux!—that has only made me more attractive to my husband; so you lost and I won there. Well, judging by certain signs, I believe you have already lost him; and you certainly intended that I should leave him—do as you did with your fiancé and regret; but, you see, I don't do that—we mustn't be too exacting. And why should I take only what no one else wants?

Perhaps, take it all in all, I am at this moment the stronger one. You received nothing from me, but you gave me much. And now I seem like a thief since you have awakened and find I possess what is your loss. How could it be otherwise when everything is worthless and sterile in your hands? You can never keep a man's love with your tulips and your passions—but I can keep it. You can't learn how to live from your authors, as I have learned. You have no little Eskil to cherish, even if your father's name was Eskil. And why are you always silent, silent, silent? I thought that was strength, but perhaps it is because you have nothing to say! Because you never think about anything! (*Rises and picks up slippers.*) Now I'm going home—and take the tulips with me—*your* tulips! You are unable to learn from another; you can't bend—therefore, you broke like a dry stalk. But I won't break! Thank you, Amelia, for all your good lessons. Thanks for teaching my husband how to love. Now I'm going home to love him. (*Goes.*)

In spite of the fact that *The Stronger* is a monologue, it is a character study not only of Mrs. X, but to a lesser extent of Miss Y and of Mrs. X's husband Bob. We can learn a good deal about these three people by making inferences from what is said. As we do this, we are also discovering much of what happened before the action of the play.

As the play begins, Mrs. X enters the cafe and comments on the apparent loneliness of Miss Y "sitting here alone on Christmas eve like a poor bachelor!" Then Mrs. X goes on with an anecdote about a bride and groom who seem not to care for one another. The story seems to suggest that no one cares for Miss Y. When the latter begins to speak, possibly to ask what the story has to do with her, Mrs. X admits that "they are not altogether the same thing."

Mrs. X then begins to speak of the past, about "him," evidently a man that Miss Y once intended to marry. Mrs. X then goes on to say that home and children are best "next to the theatre," but when she suggests that Miss Y would not understand that, the latter "looks up scornfully."

The next section of the monologue deals with the Christmas presents "for my piggywigs," a silly expression. When the toy gun goes off, there is some hint that Miss Y expected it might be real. Evidence is building that there is some tension between the two women. Mrs. X alludes to the belief that Miss Y was dropped from the Stora theatre "because I stood in your way." She quickly adds a statement of her innocence, yet says several times that Miss Y never believed in that innocence. The reader files away the thought, Was Mrs. X really innocent?

As Mrs. X carries on the pantomime and talk with the slippers, Miss Y laughs aloud at the statement, "You've never seen him [Mr. X] in slippers!" As Mr. X's grumpiness is acted out, Miss Y's laughing increases. Why? Mrs. X, after some puzzlement, says, "And you see he's true to me. . . . He told me himself." She mentions "that brazen Frederika" who, as Bob [Mr. X] told her, "wanted to seduce him." Mrs. X's reaction to this is told with a series of pauses, leading to "Frederika wasn't the only one!" Do the pauses indicate a lack of assurance?

Then we get two key sentences, "I don't know why, but the women are crazy about my husband. They must think he has influence about getting them theatrical engagements, because he is connected with the government." These lines remind us of the earlier thought, Did Mrs. X conspire to get Miss Y out of the Stora theatre? We now know that she at least had the opportunity.

Finally, in that same speech, we get a hint that possibly Miss Y was involved with Mr. X. Mrs. X did not trust her rival and speaks vaguely of a "grudge" between Bob and Miss Y. At this point the women "look at each other in a puzzled way." Mrs. X may be thinking, Am I right? Miss Y may be puzzling, How much does she know? The reader may wonder whether Bob was putting on an act?

In the next speech, ideas about the past begin to come together for Mrs. X. She begins to detail her past relations with Miss Y. When the latter visited the X's, there was "always discord." Then Miss Y became engaged to the "him" mentioned earlier in the play. Thereafter, Bob and Amelia [Miss Y] developed a "violent friendship." "I didn't get jealous," says Mrs. X, and the reader adds, I wonder if that is true? When she describes the christening and Miss Y's confusion on being kissed by Bob, Mrs. X's sentences break down into a series of broken phrases as she recalls the past. Suddenly the scattered suspicions begin to connect. She "rises suddenly" and blames Miss Y for unwinding all these suspicious thoughts that had built up in Mrs. X "like raw silk in its cocoon." Her questions, which pour out on Miss Y, suggest answers to the reader. Amelia broke her engagement because she had fallen in love with Bob. She can no longer bear seeing him. She will not go to Mrs. X's home tonight.

Mrs. X, now in possession of a truth she has long suspected, moves to another table. The word "tulips" reoccurs. She realizes why her husband "wants tulips on everything," as she said earlier in the play, why the X's go to a lake in the summer, and why her boy is named Eskil. Her fury mounts as she realizes Amelia's influence on the X's lives.

The title of the play is recalled as Mrs. X says, "The stronger I strove to keep up the deeper I worked myself down, down, . . . and there I am lying now." Mrs. X abuses Miss Y and reads many different motives into what is going on in the latter's mind. Mrs. X accuses Amelia of being the "weaker one" and says that she herself is "the stronger one." In what tone should the actress speak the last paragraph? With sarcasm? With pity? With assurance?

What is Strindberg saying? Is Amelia really the stronger for having given up Bob? Or did Bob give her up? Is Mrs. X really the stronger for going on with her present life in the light of what she knows?

EXERCISE

Write a paper discussing who is "the stronger," making clear what you mean by *stronger*. Feel free to use any ideas in the above discussion, but put them in your own words. Before you write, consider:

1. The play has one central character; if the title does not mean that she is the stronger, it must be ironic.
2. Does Mrs. X change in the course of the play?
3. The present action of the play takes place on Christmas eve, which symbolically represents a birth of love. Does that idea have any connection with the play? What character seems most capable of real love?

In making your notes, you may want to consider the following rough outline.

The past
- Reasons for tension between the women
  - The Stora theatre incident
  - Their relations with Bob

The present
- The present lives of the two women, as far as you can tell
- Characterization of Mrs. X
- Position of Miss Y
- Comment on the final paragraph, indicating what the lines mean and how they should be read by the actress

Then write your opening paragraph on what you take to be the meaning of the play.

Now write a rough draft of your paper, correct it, and make the final copy.

THE TWO MODES OF DRAMA

Drama is ordinarily discussed under two major headings: comedy and tragedy. The division is not always easy to make, given the 2,500 years in which men have written plays. Any attempt to strictly define comedy and tragedy will lead to arguments about the exceptions. But understanding what some critics have said about these two modes will help us make up our own minds as we read plays.

The essential difference is in the ways that a writer looks at the world, his own comic or tragic vision. That men can smile or laugh at life gave us comedy. That people suffer and that individuals react against suffering brought us tragedy. Both are facts of our existence. When those ideas become action, we have drama; and those plays help us to define what man can be. What we ask of the dramatist is whether his work is enjoyable and worth reading.

TRAGEDY

What is tragedy? Aristotle (384–322 B.C.), in his *Poetics*, developed a classic definition of tragedy. To sum up his ideas, we can say that tragedy is an organized presentation of human suffering. But suffering alone does not make tragedy; we must examine the causes and the effects of suffering. There are two main causes: fate, the portion of a person's life that he cannot control; and character, that which he can control and the choices that he makes in dealing with his predicament. In a tragedy, both causes should be at work, because if fate alone causes the downfall, the effect is one of pathos: we will merely pity the character. According to Aristotle, the story should be guided partly by human will. The hero in a tragedy should make some choice that brings about his own downfall, because this will evoke a feeling of both pity and terror from the audience: pity, because of the way fate overwhelms the character; and terror, because he brings defeat on himself, a human failing the audience can identify with. The ideal tragedy blends fate and character as essential ingredients. Fate sets the conditions under which the hero must act, but act he must. His action then brings about a reversal in his fortunes.

In tragic drama, then, there is always a struggle. The hero is fighting fate, but because of his own nature he cannot win. He must be strong enough to have a chance of winning or there is no action. He must have a flaw or there is no catastrophe. The catastrophe is his final defeat and usually his death.

Tragedy presents a human being in his losing struggle against circumstances and his own weakness. To know whether an incident is tragic, we must know its causes. For this reason Aristotle said that tragic drama must have a beginning, a middle, and an end. That is, the audience must know the circumstances and causes of the situation, must follow the action, and must see the catastrophe.

Usually the protagonist is a person of high rank, an exceptional man, because the odds will be better and the fall will be greater. In our pity for him and terror at his weakness, we will be emotionally relieved or freed of the small pities and fears that usually hold us. The latter idea is called catharsis or purgation. Although we feel that the suffering is outside of ourselves, through our identification with the tragic hero, as we watch, we live the experience with him.

In this way Aristotle defined tragedy, and his ideas have served us well; but modern writers and critics have to some extent modified his ideas, or at least our version of what he meant. They have argued with some of the terms used in translating Aristotle's ideas into English, claiming that some translations have been misleading. Tragedy begins when a person caught in a particular situation makes a choice, a decision to carry out some course of action. Some translators called this moment a "fatal flaw," so giving an impression of weakness in the hero. Today the term "wrong choice" is more often used. But there is also the question of whether a tragic hero, given the kind of person he is, actually has any choice that could possibly save him. He is really a man driven into a corner by a situation against which he must act, and if he is a true tragic hero, he does act. He cannot act differently without contradicting his basic character.

Writers of contemporary tragedies have changed the emphasis on some of Aristotle's definitions. Some people will argue that *Death of a Salesman* is a tragedy, even though it does not wholly conform to Aristotle's definition. One could also argue that each generation makes its own definition of tragedy. At any rate, we can make some generalizations that will apply to much of contemporary tragedy.

More emphasis is put on the environment than on what the ancients called fate. The earlier definition of fate as being the will of the gods has changed to fate as being the environment, or society, or "the system," which seems to control man's destiny. Today's tragic hero is often more passive and resigned to his fate; he does not fight back. Consequently, we are often led to wonder whether the tragedy was really inevitable.

The social class to which the tragic hero belongs has also changed: the king, prince, or "man of high estate" is often replaced by the common man, without nobility or exceptional character. Therefore the odds have changed, and the protagonist no longer seems capable of winning. The audience feels more pity than terror as it watches the action.

Finally, in Greek and Shakespearean tragedy the death of the hero marked a change in the fortunes of the state; his death mattered in changing his world. Today's heroes seem to sink unnoticed beneath the waves.

Read the following play—again as though you were playing the parts. Then turn to the discussion of how it is put together.

RIDERS TO THE SEA

John Millington Synge

Characters

MAURYA, an old woman
BARTLEY, her son
CATHLEEN, her daughter
NORA, a younger daughter
MEN and WOMEN

SCENE—*An island off the west of Ireland. Cottage kitchen, with nets, oilskins, spinning-wheel, some new boards standing by the wall, etc. CATHLEEN, a girl of about twenty, finishes kneading cake, and puts it down in the pot-oven by the fire; then wipes her hands, and begins to spin at the wheel. NORA, a young girl, puts her head in at the door.*

NORA: (*In a low voice*) Where is she?

CATHLEEN: She's lying down, God help her, and maybe sleeping, if she's able.

(*NORA comes in softly, and takes a bundle from under her shawl.*)

CATHLEEN: (*Spinning the wheel rapidly*) What is it you have?

NORA: The young priest is after bringing them. It's a shirt and a plain stocking were got off a drowned man in Donegal.

(*CATHLEEN stops her wheel with a sudden movement, and leans out to listen.*)

NORA: We're to find out if it's Michael's they are, some time herself will be down looking by the sea.

CATHLEEN: How would they be Michael's, Nora? How would he go the length of that way to the far north?

NORA: The young priest says he's known the like of it. "If it's Michael's they are," says he, "you can tell herself he's got a clean burial by the grace of God, and if they're not his, let no one say a word about them, for she'll be getting her death," says he, "with crying and lamenting."

(*The door which NORA half closed is blown open by a gust of wind.*)

CATHLEEN: (*Looking out anxiously*) Did you ask him would he stop Bartley going this day with the horses to the Galway fair?

NORA: "I won't stop him," says he, "but let you not be afraid. Herself does be saying prayers half through the night, and the Almighty God won't leave her destitute," says he, "with no son living."

CATHLEEN: Is the sea bad by the white rocks, Nora?

NORA: Middling bad. God help us. There's a great roaring in the west, and it's worse it'll be getting when the tide's turned to the wind. (*She goes over to the table with the bundle.*) Shall I open it now?

CATHLEEN: Maybe she'd wake up on us, and come in before we'd done. (*Coming to the table.*) It's a long time we'll be, and the two of us crying.

NORA: (*Goes to the inner door and listens*) She's moving about on the bed. She'll be coming in a minute.

CATHLEEN: Give me the ladder, and I'll put them up in the turf-loft, the way she won't know of them at all, and maybe when the tide turns she'll be going down to see would he be floating from the east.

(They put the ladder against the gable of the chimney; CATHLEEN goes up a few steps and hides the bundle in the turf-loft. MAURYA comes from the inner room.)

MAURYA: (*Looking up at CATHLEEN and speaking querulously*) Isn't it turf enough you have for this day and evening?

CATHLEEN: There's a cake baking at the fire for a short space (*throwing down the turf*) and Bartley will want it when the tide turns if he goes to Connemara.

(NORA picks up the turf and puts it round the pot-oven.)

MAURYA: (*Sitting down on a stool at the fire*) He won't go this day with the wind rising from the south and west. He won't go this day, for the young priest will stop him surely.

NORA: He'll not stop him, mother, and I heard Eamon Simon and Stephen Pheety and Colum Shawn saying he would go.

MAURYA: Where is he itself?

NORA: He went down to see would there be another boat sailing in the week, and I'm thinking it won't be long till he's here now, for the tide's turning at the green head, and the hooker's [1] tacking from the east.

CATHLEEN: I hear someone passing the big stones.

NORA: (*Looking out*) He's coming now, and he in a hurry.

BARTLEY: (*Comes in and looks round the room; speaking sadly and quietly*) Where is the bit of new rope, Cathleen, which was bought in Connemara?

CATHLEEN: (*Coming down*) Give it to him, Nora; it's on a nail by the white boards. I hung it up this morning, for the pig with the black feet was eating it.

NORA: (*Giving him a rope*) Is that it, Bartley?

MAURYA: You'd do right to leave that rope, Bartley, hanging by the boards. (*BARTLEY takes the rope.*) It will be wanting in this place, I'm telling you, if Michael is washed up tomorrow morning, or the next morning, or

1. hooker: sailing vessel.

any morning in the week, for it's a deep grave we'll make him by the grace of God.

BARTLEY: (*Beginning to work with the rope*) I've no halter the way I can ride down on the mare, and I must go now quickly. This is the one boat going for two weeks or beyond it, and the fair will be a good fair for horses I heard them saying below.

MAURYA: It's a hard thing they'll be saying below if the body is washed up and there's no man in it to make the coffin, and I after giving a big price for the finest white boards you'd find in Connemara.

(*She looks round at the boards.*)

BARTLEY: How would it be washed up, and we after looking each day for nine days, and a strong wind blowing a while back from the west and south?

MAURYA: If it wasn't found itself, that wind is raising the sea, and there was a star up against the moon, and it rising in the night. If it was a hundred horses, or a thousand horses you had itself, what is the price of a thousand horses against a son where there is one son only?

BARTLEY: (*Working at the halter, to CATHLEEN*) Let you go down each day, and see the sheep aren't jumping in on the rye, and if the jobber comes you can sell the pig with the black feet if there is a good price going.

MAURYA: How would the like of her get a good price for a pig?

BARTLEY: (*To CATHLEEN*) If the west wind holds with the last bit of the moon let you and Nora get up weed enough for another cock for the kelp. It's hard set we'll be from this day with no one in it but one man to work.

MAURYA: It's hard set we'll be surely the day you're drownd'd with the rest. What way will I live and the girls with me, and I an old woman looking for the grave?

(*BARTLEY lays down the halter, takes off his old coat, and puts on a newer one of the same flannel.*)

BARTLEY: (*To NORA*) Is she coming to the pier?

NORA: (*Looking out*) She's passing the green head and letting fall her sails.

BARTLEY: (*Getting his purse and tobacco*) I'll have

half an hour to go down, and you'll see me coming again in two days, or in three days, or maybe in four days if the wind is bad.

MAURYA (*Turning round to the fire, and putting her shawl over her head*) Isn't it a hard and cruel man won't hear a word from an old woman, and she holding him from the sea?

CATHLEEN: It's the life of a young man to be going on the sea, and who would listen to an old woman with one thing and she saying it over?

BARTLEY: (*Taking the halter*) I must go now quickly. I'll ride down on the red mare, and the gray pony'll run behind me. . . . The blessing of God on you. (*He goes out.*)

MAURYA: (*Crying out as he is in the door*) He's gone now, God spare us, and we'll not see him again. He's gone now, and when the black night is falling I'll have no son left me in the world.

CATHLEEN: Why wouldn't you give him your blessing and he looking round in the door? Isn't it sorrow enough is on every one in this house without your sending him out with an unlucky word behind him, and a hard word in his ear?

(*MAURYA takes up the tongs and begins raking the fire aimlessly without looking round.*)

NORA: (*Turning toward her*) You're taking away the turf from the cake.

CATHLEEN: (*Crying out*) The Son of God forgive us, Nora, we're after forgetting his bit of bread.

(*She comes over to the fire.*)

NORA: And it's destroyed he'll be going till dark night, and he after eating nothing since the sun went up.

CATHLEEN: (*Turning the cake out of the oven*) It's destroyed he'll be, surely. There's no sense left on any person in a house where an old woman will be talking forever.

(*MAURYA sways herself on her stool.*)

CATHLEEN: (*Cutting off some of the bread and rolling it in a cloth; to MAURYA*) Let you go down to the spring well and give him this and he passing. You'll see him then and the dark word will be broken, and you can say "God speed you," the way he'll be easy in his mind.

MAURYA (*Taking the bread*) Will I be in it as soon as himself?

CATHLEEN: If you go now quickly.

MAURYA: (*Standing up unsteadily*) It's hard set I am to walk.

CATHLEEN: (*Looking at her anxiously*) Give her the stick, Nora, or maybe she'll slip on the big stones.

NORA: What stick?

CATHLEEN: The stick Michael brought from Connemara.

MAURYA: (*Taking a stick NORA gives her*) In the big world the old people do be leaving things after them for their sons and children, but in this place it is the young men do be leaving things behind for them that do be old.

(*She goes out slowly. NORA goes over to the ladder.*)

CATHLEEN: Wait, Nora, maybe she'd turn back quickly. She's that sorry. God help her, you wouldn't know the thing she'd do.

NORA: Is she gone round by the bush?

CATHLEEN: (*Looking out*) She's gone now. Throw it down quickly, for the Lord knows when she'll be out of it again.

NORA: (*Getting the bundle from the loft*) The young priest said he'd be passing tomorrow, and we might go down and speak to him below if it's Michael's they are surely.

CATHLEEN: (*Taking the bundle*) Did he say what way they were found?

NORA: (*Coming down*) "There were two men," says he, "and they rowing round with poteen before the cocks crowed, and the oar of one of them caught the body, and they passing the black cliffs of the north."

CATHLEEN: (*Trying to open the bundle*) Give me a knife, Nora, the string's perished with the salt water, and there's a black knot on it you wouldn't loosen in a week.

NORA: (*Giving her a knife*) I've heard tell it was a long way to Donegal.

CATHLEEN: (*Cutting the string*) It is surely. There was

a man in here a while ago—the man sold us that knife—and he said if you set off walking from the rocks beyond, it would be seven days you'd be in Donegal.

NORA: And what time would a man take, and he floating?

(*CATHLEEN opens the bundle and takes out a bit of a stocking. They look at them eagerly.*)

CATHLEEN: (*In a low voice*) The Lord spare us, Nora! isn't it a queer hard thing to say if it's his they are surely?

NORA: I'll get his shirt off the hook the way we can put the one flannel on the other. (*She looks through some clothes hanging in the corner.*) It's not with them, Cathleen, and where will it be?

CATHLEEN: I'm thinking Bartley put it on him in the morning, for his own shirt was heavy with the salt in it. (*Pointing to the corner.*) There's a bit of a sleeve was of the same stuff. Give me that and it will do.

(*NORA brings it to her and they compare the flannel.*)

CATHLEEN: It's the same stuff, Nora; but if it is itself aren't there great rolls of it in the shops of Galway, and isn't it many another man may have a shirt of it as well as Michael himself?

NORA: (*Who has taken up the stocking and counted the stitches, crying out*) It's Michael, Cathleen, it's Michael; God spare his soul, and what will herself say when she hears this story, and Bartley on the sea?

CATHLEEN: (*Taking the stocking*) It's a plain stocking.

NORA: It's the second one of the third pair I knitted, and I put up threescore stitches, and I dropped four of them.

CATHLEEN: (*Counts the stitches*) It's that number is in it. (*Crying out.*) Ah, Nora, isn't it a bitter thing to think of him floating that way to the far north, and no one to keen him but the black hags that do be flying on the sea?

NORA: (*Swinging herself round, and throwing out her arms on the clothes*) And isn't it a pitiful thing when there is nothing left of a man who was a great rower and fisher, but a bit of an old shirt and a plain stocking?

CATHLEEN: (*After an instant*) Tell me is herself coming, Nora? I hear a little sound on the path.

NORA: (*Looking out*) She is, Cathleen. She's coming up to the door.

CATHLEEN: Put these things away before she'll come in. Maybe it's easier she'll be after giving her blessing to Bartley, and we won't let on we've heard anything the time he's on the sea.

NORA: (*Helping CATHLEEN to close the bundle*) We'll put them here in the corner.

(*They put them into a hole in the chimney corner. CATHLEEN goes back to the spinning-wheel.*)

NORA: Will she see it was crying I was?

CATHLEEN: Keep your back to the door the way the light'll not be on you.

(*NORA sits down at the chimney corner, with her back to the door. MAURYA comes in very slowly, without looking at the girls, and goes over to her stool at the other side of the fire. The cloth with the bread still in her hand. The girls look at each other, and NORA points to the bundle of bread.*)

CATHLEEN: (*After spinning for a moment*) You didn't give him his bit of bread?

(*MAURYA begins to keen softly, without turning round.*)

CATHLEEN: Did you see him riding down? (*MAURYA goes on keening.*)

CATHLEEN: (*A little impatiently*) God forgive you; isn't it a better thing to raise your voice and tell what you seen, than to be making lamentation for a thing that's done? Did you see Bartley, I'm saying to you.

MAURYA: (*With a weak voice*) My heart's broken from this day.

CATHLEEN: (*As before*) Did you see Bartley?

MAURYA: I seen the fearfulest thing.

CATHLEEN: (*Leaves her wheel and looks out*) God forgive you; he's riding the mare now over the green head, and the gray pony behind him.

MAURYA: (*Starts, so that her shawl falls back from her head and shows her white tossed hair; with a frightened voice*) The gray pony behind him. . . .

CATHLEEN: (*Coming to the fire*) What is it ails you at all?

MAURYA: (*Speaking very slowly*) I've seen the fearfulest thing any person has seen, since the day Bride Dara seen the dead man with a child in his arms.

CATHLEEN AND NORA: Uah.

(*They crouch down in front of the old woman at the fire.*)

NORA: Tell us what it is you seen.

MAURYA: I went down to the spring well, and I stood there saying a payer to myself. Then Bartley came along, and he riding on the red mare with the gray pony behind him. (*She puts up her hands, as if to hide something from her eyes.*) The Son of God spare us, Nora!

CATHLEEN: What is it you seen?

MAURYA: I seen Michael himself.

CATHLEEN: (*Speaking softly*) You did not, mother; it wasn't Michael you seen, for his body is after being found in the far north, and he's got a clean burial, by the grace of God.

MAURYA: (*A little defiantly*) I'm after seeing him this day, and he riding and galloping. Bartley came first on the red mare; and I tried to say, "God speed you," but something choked the words in my throat. He went by quickly; and "the blessing of God on you," says he, and I could say nothing. I looked up then, and I crying, at the gray pony, and there was Michael upon it—with fine clothes on him, and new shoes on his feet.

CATHLEEN: (*Begins to keen*) It's destroyed we are from this day. It's destroyed, surely.

NORA: Didn't the young priest say the Almighty God wouldn't leave her destitute with no son living?

MAURYA: (*In a low voice, but clearly*) It's little the like of him knows of the sea. . . . Bartley will be lost now, and let you call in Eamon and make me a good coffin out of the white boards, for I won't live after them. I've had a husband, and a husband's father, and six sons in this house—six fine men, though it was a hard birth I had with every one of them and they coming to the world—and some of them were found and some of them were not found, but they're gone now the lot of them. . . . There were Stephen, and Shawn, were lost in the great wind, and found after in the Bay of Gregory of the Golden Mouth, and carried up the two of them on the one plank, and in by that door.

(*She pauses for a moment; the girls start as if they heard something through the door that is half open behind them.*)

NORA: (*In a whisper*) Did you hear that, Cathleen? Did you hear a noise in the northeast?

CATHLEEN: (*Continues without hearing anything*) There was Sheamus and his father, and his own father again, were lost in a dark night, and not a stick or sign was seen of them when the sun went up. There was Patch after was drowned out of a curagh that turned over. I was sitting here with Bartley, and he a baby, lying on my two knees, and I seen two women, and three women, and four women coming in, and they crossing themselves, and not saying a word. I looked out then, and there were men coming after them, and they holding a thing in the half of a red sail, and water dripping out of it—it was a dry day, Nora—and leaving a track to the door.

(*She pauses again with her hand stretched out toward the door. It opens softly and old women begin to come in, crossing themselves on the threshold, and kneeling down in front of the stage with red petticoats over their heads.*)

MAURYA: (*Half in a dream, to CATHLEEN*) Is it Patch, or Michael, or what is it at all?

CATHLEEN: Michael is after being found in the far north, and when he is found there how could he be here in this place?

MAURYA: There does be a power of young men floating round in the sea, and what way would they know if it was Michael they had, or another man like him, for when a man is nine days in the sea, and the wind blowing, it's hard set his own mother would be to say what man was it.

CATHLEEN: It's Michael, God spare him, for they're after sending us a bit of his clothes from the far north.

(*She reaches out and hands MAURYA the clothes that belonged to MICHAEL. MAURYA stands up slowly, and takes them in her hands. NORA looks out.*)

NORA: They're carrying a thing among them and there's water dripping out of it and leaving a track by the big stones.

CATHLEEN: (*In a whisper to the women who have come in*) Is it Bartley it is?

ONE OF THE WOMEN: It is, surely, God rest his soul.

(*Two younger women come in and pull out the table. Then men carry in the body of BARTLEY, laid on a plank, with a bit of a sail over it, and lay it on the table.*)

CATHLEEN: (*To the women, as they are doing so*) What way was he drowned?

ONE OF THE WOMEN: The gray pony knocked him into the sea, and he was washed out where there is a great surf on the white rocks.

(*MAURYA has gone over and knelt down at the head of the table. The women are keening softly and swaying themselves with a slow movement. CATHLEEN and NORA kneel at the other end of the table. The men kneel near the door.*)

MAURYA: (*Raising her head and speaking as if she did not see the people around her*) They're all gone now, and there isn't anything more the sea can do to me. . . . I'll have no call now to be up crying and praying when the wind breaks from the south, and you can hear the surf is in the east, and the surf is in the west, making a great stir with the two noises, and they hitting one on the other. I'll have no call now to be going down and getting holy water in the dark nights after Samhain,[2] and I won't care what way the sea is when the other women will be keening. (*To NORA.*) Give me the holy water, Nora; there's a small sup still on the dresser.

MAURYA: (*Drops MICHAEL'S clothes across BARTLEY'S feet, and sprinkles the holy water over him*) It isn't that I haven't prayed for you, Bartley, to the Almighty God. It isn't that I haven't said prayers in the dark night till you wouldn't know what I'd be saying; but it's a great rest I'll have now, and it's time surely. It's a great rest I'll have now, and great sleeping in the long nights after Sam-

2. Samhain: feast of All Saints, November 1.

hain, if it's only a bit of wet flour we do have to eat, and maybe a fish that would be stinking.

(*She kneels down again, crossing herself, and saying prayers under her breath.*)

CATHLEEN: (*To an old man*) Maybe yourself and Eamon would make a coffin when the sun rises. We have fine white boards herself bought, God help her, thinking Michael would be found, and I have a new cake you can eat while you'll be working.

THE OLD MAN: (*Looking at the boards*) Are there nails with them?

CATHLEEN: There are not, Colum; we didn't think of the nails.

ANOTHER MAN: It's a great wonder she wouldn't think of the nails, and all the coffins she's seen made already.

CATHLEEN: It's getting old she is, and broken.

(*MAURYA stands up again very slowly and spreads out the pieces of MICHAEL'S clothes beside the body, sprinkling them with the last of the holy water.*)

NORA: (*In a whisper to CATHLEEN*) She's quiet now and easy; but the day Michael was drowned you could hear her crying out from this to the spring well. It's fonder she was of Michael, and would any one have thought that?

CATHLEEN: (*Slowly and clearly*) An old woman will be soon tired with anything she will do, and isn't it nine days herself is after crying and keening, and making great sorrow in the house?

MAURYA: (*Puts the empty cup, mouth downwards, on the table, and lays her hands together on BARTLEY'S feet*) They're all together this time, and the end is come. May the Almighty God have mercy on Bartley's soul, and on Michael's soul, and on the souls of Sheamus and Patch, and Stephen and Shawn; (*bending her head*) and may he have mercy on my soul, Nora, and on the soul of every one is left living in the world.

(*She pauses, and the keen rises a little more loudly from the women, then sinks away.*)

MAURYA: (*Continuing*) Michael has a clean burial in the far north, by the grace of the Almighty God. Bartley will have a fine coffin out of the white boards, and a deep grave surely. What more can we want than that? No man at all can be living forever, and we must be satisfied.

(She kneels down again and the curtain falls slowly.)

Riders to the Sea, first performed in 1904, is considered the best one-act tragedy in English. Set in the Aran Islands off the west coast of Ireland, the play is based on man's struggle for existence; specifically, it depicts the final stages of Maurya's defeat by the power of the sea.

Pared to essentials, the play seems at first glance simpler than it is. Two major qualities stand out immediately: the poetic diction that Synge has made of Irish peasant speech, and the ritual quality of the action. The rhythmic language, though not written as verse lines, adds a poetic quality and intensity to the play. The drama moves like a ritual as the characters confront their fate, culminating in the bringing in of Bartley's body, the gathering of the neighbors, and the mourning for the dead. There is no suspense; a tragic vision shrouds the action from the beginning. The play is showing how people face a fate that is inevitable.

The major conflict is between Maurya's family and the ever-present threat of death by drowning, symbolized by the cottage and the sea. In our first view of the kitchen, the nets and oilskins bring to our attention the sea and the men who sail on it. The spinning wheel and the presence of three women in the house call to mind the personification of the Fates in Greek mythology, who controlled the distribution of good and evil to mankind. The Fates (Moirae) were represented as three women: Clotho, who spun the web of life into a cloth representing the acts of a man's life; Lachesis, who measured the length of that life; and Atropos, who cut the thread, so marking the end of life. Their weaving is a metaphor for the development of a man's life. What they weave is a cloth tapestry in which man's life is portrayed. At any moment the thread may be cut. The suggestion, of course, is that man does not control his own destiny. The women in the play, too, are trying to control fate, but they ironically fail. The metaphoric meaning is reinforced when Cathleen cuts the "black knot" that holds Michael's clothes.

In the opening scene, then, the author represents for us the three basic forces in the play: the home, the sea, and fate.

The exposition is a model of economy. The play begins with a question about Maurya, "Where is she?" At the end of the play, as we listen to Maurya's final comments, we can consider the same question, though it is not repeated. In the first nine speeches we learn that Nora has a shirt and stockings given to her by the young priest and taken from the body of a drowned man found afloat at Donegal. Do they belong to their brother Michael for whom their mother has been mourning for nine days? We also learn that Bartley is planning to leave the island that day to take horses to the Galway fair. Finally, in this brief span of time, we hear the priest's promise about Maurya, ". . . the Almighty God won't leave her destitute, with no son living." A Christian idea enters again, when Maurya "sees" Michael, in an obvious reference to Revelation (VI, 8), "And I looked, and behold a pale horse; and his name that sat on him was Death."

But the play is close to the old pagan beliefs that still persist in the islands. Michael was drowned at Samhain (Sòw-en), Hallowe'en, the time that marks the end of the harvest and the beginning of the barren season. It also marks the pagan festival of the dead, when ghosts return; and, ironically in the play, it marks the beginning of the Celtic year. In many early myths, a cake of dough (bread) is a traditional offering to the gods, to secure their favor. The pagan influence is further seen in the keening, an ancient wailing lamentation for the dead. This choral expression of grief supports the ritual quality of the play, and a function of ritual is to help man endure his suffering.

The play, then, is a metaphoric statement of every man's struggle for existence, and it deals with the last day of Maurya's struggle against the sea. It draws no moral judgment, for no choice is offered to these people. Maurya bows to the will of the gods. Christianity offers no solution: the priest never even enters the cottage, and his predictions are not sustained. When the end comes, Maurya can only turn down the empty cup and ask for mercy. The dead will be buried—"What more can we want than that? No man at all can be living forever, and we must be satisfied."

EXERCISE

Write an essay on the play, showing how the various recurring ideas (motifs) contribute to the theme. Then comment on the elements of tragedy you find in the play. Pay particular attention to the following motifs:

The use of colors as related to death
Red (the red mare, the red petticoats of the mourners, the red sail in which Patch was wrapped)
White (the boards for the coffin, the color of rocks)
Water as a symbol of death (references to the spring well, the sea, water dripping from Patch's body, the Holy water)
The handing on of articles (Michael's clothes, Bartley's taking Michael's new shirt, Maurya's use of Michael's stick, the grave rope taken as a halter)
Allusions to fate (three women and the spinning wheel, cutting of the "black knot," the "dropped stitches in the stockings)
Allusion to the line from Revelation ("And I looked, and behold a pale horse; and his name that sat on him was Death.")
Time of Michael's death (Samhain, Hallowe'en, the time when ghosts of the dead return)
The function of the comments of the young priest

Reread the section on tragedy and decide how well the play fits the definitions of tragedy that you find there. Add your own ideas, along with supportive evidence, in the last portion of your paper.

COMEDY

If a writer intends to reform human behavior, he can do it best by writing comedy; few people like to be thought of as being funny. George Meredith described humor as carrying the "Sword of Common Sense" with which the writer attacks deviations from common sense. The comic spirit has a moral purpose in "teaching the world what ails it," and in giving rise to "thoughtful laughter."

Comedy, then, is intended to reform. Its appeal is not to the emotions, but rather to the intellect, in the catching of incongruities in man's actions. It demands in an audience what the

French philosopher Henri Bergson called "momentary anaesthesia of the heart." And Horace Walpole's statement, made in the eighteenth century, is still true: "The world is a comedy to those that think, a tragedy to those who feel."

A traditional concern of comedy is in analyzing self-deception as it cuts through the roles we play in life and gets at who we really are. Comedy is not merely laughable, but one of the richest ways man has to discover his own nature. It can help man to see himself in a clearer perspective by emphasizing the humanness of his folly. A study of comedy thus helps one to see himself as part of a larger social group, as opposed to an isolated individual.

A final reason for comedy is that it portrays an optimistic view of the world. The rituals of primitive man still appear in our dramatic art because they reflect persisting aspects of human nature. They repeat a cycle of struggle, death, and resurrection. Tragedy is concerned with the first half of the struggle, that leading to defeat; comedy, with the last half, the purgation and triumph. Laughter liberates us; it suggests what we ought to be.

Great comedy, then, should be the story of achievement. At the end the hero should be still on his feet. The comic view, through all myth and legend, does not contradict man's defeat, but rather transcends it. It admits that man may take a beating, but points out also that he can rise above it.

The word *comedy* derives from the Greek word *komos* meaning revel, especially that involved in the festivals in honor of Dionysus, the god of wine and revelry. Beginning as a procession of singing, dancing, and banter, it was regularized in play form by the Greek playwright Aristophanes, who lived about 448–388 B.C. In his plays, such as *The Birds* or *The Clouds*, simple stories became satires. Characters were mere caricatures or symbols for abstract ideas. They wore masks of easily recognized types and were often grotesque and extravagantly padded.

Two major traditions of stage comedy have persisted in English. Ben Jonson's bitter comedies, written at the time of Shakespeare, are one type. The characters are dominated by a single trait or "humor": greed, gluttony, hypocrisy. Single-minded and predictable, they become machinelike and therefore ridiculous. Manipulating the hero toward an ignoble end is a knave, who is a minor character. In this type of comedy, almost all the characters are exposed for what they really are and judged, and we are happy to see justice done. The characters do not change or reform, and society is not changed by what happens in the play. This type of formula continues on television today. Shakespearean comedy, representing the other tradition, is more romantic; it is a "comedy of atonement." The characters have a number of traits and are sometimes complex and unpredictable. The divided society, often represented as a split in a family, is reconciled by the play's end, at least for the major characters.

Comedy makes use of the "invented plot," as some critics have called it, another element that separates it from tragedy. In comedy we do not see the tight cause and effect relations that lead a tragic character toward doom. The relation of scenes in a comedy is often manipulated—thought out as a joke, it succeeds as a joke.

A comic scene may exemplify the term *sudden glory*, the moment in which the audience glories in their own superiority, being quite sure that they would not have acted as the comic character did. Ridicule works best when the author convinces us that the object of ridicule is inferior to us, the audience. Such a scene may also reflect Aristotle's idea of relaxation of concern: excitement may be built up and then be relieved by laughter. But even as we indulge in "thoughtful laughter," we often find that we are laughing at our own weaknesses as they are portrayed on the stage.

Read the following play and the discussion about how it works.

THE BRUTE

Anton Chekhov

A Joke in One Act

English Version by Eric Bentley

Characters

MRS. POPOV, widow and landowner, small, with dimpled cheeks.

MR. GRIGORY S. SMIRNOV, gentleman farmer, middle-aged.
LUKA, Mrs. Popov's footman, an old man.
GARDENER
COACHMAN
HIRED MEN

The drawing room of a country house. MRS. POPOV, in deep mourning, is staring hard at a photograph. LUKA is with her.

LUKA: It's not right, ma'am, you're killing yourself. The cook has gone off with the maid to pick berries. The cat's having a high old time in the yard catching birds. Every living thing is happy. But you stay moping here in the house like it was a convent, taking no pleasure in nothing. I mean it, ma'am! It must be a full year since you set foot out of doors.

MRS. POPOV: I must never set foot out of doors again, Luka. Never! I have nothing to set foot out of doors *for.* My life is done. *He* is in his grave. I have buried myself alive in this house. We are *both* in our graves.

LUKA: You're off again, ma'am. I just won't listen to you no more. Mr. Popov is dead, but what can we do about that? It's God's doing. God's will be done. You've cried over him, you've done your share of mourning, haven't you? There's a limit to everything. You can't go on weeping and wailing forever. My old lady died, for that matter, and I wept and wailed over her a whole month long. Well, that was it. I couldn't weep and wail all my life, she just wasn't worth it. (*He sighs.*) As for the neighbours, you've forgotten all about them, ma'am. You don't

---

visit them and you don't let them visit you. You and I are like a pair of spiders—excuse the expression, ma'am—here we are in this house like a pair of spiders, we never see the light of day. And it isn't like there was no nice people around either. The whole county's swarming with 'em. There's a regiment quartered at Riblov, and the officers are so good-looking! The girls can't take their eyes off them—There's a ball at the camp every Friday—The military band plays most every day of the week—What do you say, ma'am? You're young, you're pretty, you could enjoy yourself! Ten years from now you may want to strut and show your feathers to the officers, and it'll be too late.

MRS. POPOV: (*firmly*) You must never bring this subject up again, Luka. Since Popov died, life has been an empty dream to me, you know that. *You* may think I am alive. Poor ignorant Luka! You are wrong. I am dead. I'm in my grave. Never more shall I see the light of day, never strip from my body this . . . raiment of death! Are you listening, Luka? Let his ghost learn how I love him! Yes, *I* know, and *you* know, he was often unfair to me, he was cruel to me, and he was unfaithful to me. What of it? *I* shall be faithful to *him,* that's all. I will show him how *I* can love. Hereafter, in a better world than this, he will welcome me back, the same loyal girl I always was—

LUKA: Instead of carrying on this way, ma'am, you should go out in the garden and take a bit of a walk, ma'am. Or why not harness Toby and take a drive? Call on a couple of the neighbours, ma'am?

MRS. POPOV: (*breaking down*) Oh, Luka!

LUKA: Yes, ma'am? What have I said, ma'am? Oh dear!

MRS. POPOV: Toby! You said Toby! He adored that horse. When he drove me out to the Korchagins and the Vlasovs, it was always with Toby! He was a wonderful driver, do you remember, Luka? So graceful! So strong! I can see him now, pulling at those reins with all his might and main! Toby! Luka, tell them to give Toby an extra portion of oats today.

LUKA: Yes, ma'am.

(*A bell rings.*)

MRS. POPOV: Who is that? Tell them I'm not at home.

LUKA: Very good, ma'am. (*Exit.*)

MRS. POPOV: (*gazing again at the photograph*) You shall see, my Popov, how a wife can love and forgive. Till death do us part. Longer than that. Till death re-unite us forever! (*Suddenly a titter breaks through her tears.*) Aren't you ashamed of yourself, Popov? Here's your little wife, being good, being faithful, so faithful she's locked up here waiting for her own funeral, while you—doesn't it make you ashamed, you naughty boy? You were terrible, you know. You were unfaithful, and you made those awful scenes about it, you stormed out and left me alone for weeks—

(*Enter LUKA.*)

LUKA: (*upset*) There's someone asking for you, ma'am. Says he must—

MRS. POPOV: I suppose you told him that since my husband's death I see no one?

LUKA: Yes, ma'am. I did, ma'am. But he wouldn't listen, ma'am. He says it's urgent.

MRS. POPOV: (*shrilly*) I see no one!!

LUKA: He won't take no for an answer, ma'am. He just curses and swears and comes in anyway. He's a perfect monster, ma'am. He's in the dining room right now.

MRS. POPOV: In the dining room, is he? I'll give him his come uppance. Bring him in here this minute.

(*Exit LUKA.*)

(*Suddenly sad again.*) Why do they do this to me? Why? Insulting my grief, intruding on my solitude? (*She sighs.*) I'm afraid I'll have to enter a convent. I will, I *must* enter a convent!

(*Enter MR. SMIRNOV and LUKA.*)

SMIRNOV: (*to LUKA*) Dolt! Idiot! You talk too much! (*Seeing MRS. POPOV. With dignity.*) May I have the honour of introducing myself, madam? Gregory S. Smirnov, landowner and lieutenant of artillery, retired. Forgive me, madam, if I disturb your peace and quiet, but my business is both urgent and weighty.

MRS. POPOV: (*declining to offer him her hand*) What is it you wish, sir?

SMIRNOV: At the time of his death, your late husband —with whom I had the honour to be acquainted, ma'am— was in my debt to the tune of twelve hundred rubles. I have two notes to prove it. Tomorrow, ma'am, I must pay the interest on a bank loan. I have therefore no alternative, ma'am, but to ask you to pay me the money today.

MRS. POPOV: Twelve hundred rubles? But what did my husband owe it to you for?

SMIRNOV: He used to buy his oats from me, madam.

MRS. POPOV: (*to LUKA, with a sigh*) Remember what I said, Luka: tell them to give Toby an extra portion of oats today!

(*Exit LUKA.*)

My dear Mr.—what was the name again?

SMIRNOV: Smirnov, ma'am.

MRS. POPOV: My dear Mr. Smirnov, if Mr. Popov owed you money, you shall be paid—to the last ruble, to the last kopeck. But today—you must excuse me, Mr.—what was it?

SMIRNOV: Smirnov, ma'am.

MRS. POPOV: Today, Mr. Smirnov, I have no ready cash in the house.

(*SMIRNOV starts to speak.*)

Tomorrow, Mr. Smirnov, no, the day after tomorrow, all will be well. My steward will be back from town. I shall see that he pays what is owing. Today, no. In any case, today is exactly seven months from Mr. Popov's death. On such a day you will understand that I am in no mood to think of money.

SMIRNOV: Madam, if you don't pay up now, you can carry me out feet foremost. They'll seize my estate.

MRS. POPOV: You can have your money.

(*He starts to thank her.*)

Tomorrow.

(*He again starts to speak.*)

That is: the day after tomorrow.

SMIRNOV: I don't need the money the day after tomorrow. I need it today.

MRS. POPOV: I'm sorry, Mr.—

SMIRNOV: (*shouting*) Smirnov!

MRS. POPOV: (*sweetly*) Yes, of course. But you can't have it today.

SMIRNOV: But I can't wait for it any longer!

MRS. POPOV: Be sensible, Mr. Smirnov. How can I pay you if I don't have it?

SMIRNOV. You don't have it?

MRS. POPOV: I don't have it.

SMIRNOV: Sure?

MRS. POPOV: Positive.

SMIRNOV: Very well. I'll make a note to that effect. (*Shrugging.*) And then they want me to keep cool. I meet the tax commissioner on the street, and he says, "Why are you always in such a bad humour, Smirnov?" Bad humour! How can I help it, in God's name? I need money, I need it desperately. Take yesterday: I leave home at the crack of dawn, I call on all my debtors. Not a one of them pays up. Footsore and weary, I creep at midnight into some little dive, and try to snatch a few winks of sleep on the floor by the vodka barrel. Then today, I come here, fifty miles from home, saying to myself, 'At last, at last, I can be sure of something,' and you're not in the mood! You give me a mood! Christ, how can I help getting all worked up?

MRS. POPOV: I thought I'd made it clear, Mr. Smirnov, that you'll get your money the minute my steward is back from town?

SMIRNOV: What the hell do I care about your steward? Pardon the expression, ma'am. But it was you I came to see.

MRS. POPOV: What language! What a tone to take to a lady! I refuse to hear another word. (*Quickly, exit.*)

SMIRNOV: Not in the mood, huh? "Exactly seven months since Popov's death," huh? How about me? (*Shouting after her.*) Is there this interest to pay, or isn't there? I'm asking you a question: is there this interest to pay, or isn't there? So your husband died, and you're not in the mood, and your steward's gone off some place, and so forth and so on, but what *I* can do about all that, huh? What do *you* think I should do? Take a running jump and shove my head through the wall? Take off in a balloon? You don't know my *other* debtors. I call on Gruzdeff. Not at home. I look for Yaroshevitch. He's hiding out. I find Kooritsin. He kicks up a row, and I have to throw him through the window. I work my way right down the list. Not a kopeck. Then I come to you, and God damn it to hell, if you'll pardon the expression, you're not in the mood! (*Quietly, as he realizes he's talking to air.*) I've spoiled them all, that's what, I've let them play me for a sucker. Well, I'll show them. I'll show this one. I'll stay right here till she pays up. Ugh! (*He shudders with rage.*) I'm in a rage! I'm in a positively towering rage! Every nerve in my body is trembling at forty to the dozen! I can't breathe, I feel ill, I think I'm going to faint, hey, you there!

(*Enter* LUKA.)

LUKA: Yes, sir? Is there anything you wish, sir?

SMIRNOV: Water! Water! No, make it vodka.

(*Exit LUKA.*)

Consider the logic of it. A fellow creature is desperately in need of cash, so desperately in need that he has to seriously contemplate hanging himself, and this woman, this mere chit of a girl, won't pay up, and why not? Because, forsooth, she isn't in the mood! Oh, the logic of women! Come to that, I never have liked them, I could do without the whole sex. Talk to a woman? I'd rather sit on a barrel of dynamite, the very thought gives me gooseflesh. Women! Creatures of poetry and romance! Just to see one in the distance gets me mad. My legs start twitching with rage. I feel like yelling for help.

(*Enter LUKA, handing SMIRNOV a glass of water.*)

LUKA: Mrs. Popov is indisposed, sir. She is seeing no one.

SMIRNOV: Get out.

(*Exit LUKA.*)

Indisposed, is she? Seeing no one, huh? Well, she can see me or not, but I'll be here, I'll be right here till she pays up. If you're sick for a week, I'll be here for a week. If you're sick for a year, I'll be here for a year. You won't get around *me* with your widow's weeds and your schoolgirl dimples. I know all about dimples. (*Shouting through the window.*) Semyon, let the horses out of those shafts, we're not leaving, we're staying, and tell them to give the horses some oats, yes, oats, you fool, what do you think! (*Walking away from the window.*) What a mess, what an unholy mess! I didn't sleep last night, the heat is terrific today, not a damn one of 'em has paid up, and here's this—this skirt in mourning that's not in the mood! My head aches, where's that—(*He drinks from the glass.*) Water, ugh! You there!

(*Enter LUKA.*)

LUKA: Yes, sir. You wish for something, sir?

SMIRNOV: Where's that confounded vodka I asked for?

(*Exit LUKA.*)

(*SMIRNOV sits and looks himself over.*) Oof! A fine figure of a man *I* am! Unwashed, uncombed, unshaven, straw on my vest, dust all over me. The little woman must've taken me for a highwayman. (*Yawns.*) I suppose it wouldn't be considered polite to barge into a drawing room in this state, but who cares? I'm not a visitor, I'm a creditor—most unwelcome of guests, second only to Death.

(*Enter LUKA.*)

LUKA: (*handing him the vodka*) If I may say so, sir, you take too many liberties, sir.

SMIRNOV: What?!

LUKA: Oh, nothing, sir, nothing.

SMIRNOV: Who in hell do you think you're talking to? Shut your mouth!

LUKA: (*aside*) There's an evil spirit abroad. The Devil must have sent him. Oh! (*Exit LUKA.*)

SMIRNOV: What a rage I'm in! I'll grind the whole world to powder. Oh, I feel ill again. You there!

(*Enter MRS. POPOV.*)

MRS. POPOV: (*looking at the floor*) In the solitude of my rural retreat, Mr. Smirnov, I've long since grown unaccustomed to the sound of the human voice. Above all,

I cannot bear shouting. I must beg you not to break the silence.

SMIRNOV: Very well. Pay me my money and I'll go.

MRS. POPOV: I told you before, and I tell you again, Mr. Smirnov. I have no cash, you'll have to wait till the day after tomorrow. Can I express myself more plainly?

SMIRNOV: And *I* told *you* before, and *I* tell *you* again, that I need the money today, that the day after tomorrow is too late, and that if you don't pay, and pay now, I'll have to hang myself in the morning!

MRS. POPOV: But I have no cash. This is quite a puzzle.

SMIRNOV: You won't pay, huh?

MRS. POPOV: I *can't* pay, Mr. Smirnov.

SMIRNOV: In that case, I'm going to sit here and wait. (*Sits down.*) You'll pay up the day after tomorrow? Very good. Till the day after tomorrow, here I sit. (*Pause. He jumps up.*) Now look, do I have to pay that interest tomorrow, or don't I? Or do you think I'm joking?

MRS. POPOV: I must ask you not to raise your voice, Mr. Smirnov. This is not a stable.

SMIRNOV: Who said it was? Do I have to pay the interest tomorrow or not?

MRS. POPOV: Mr. Smirnov, do you know how to behave in the presence of a lady?

SMIRNOV: No, madam, I do not know how to behave in the presence of a lady.

MRS. POPOV: Just what I thought. I look at you, and I say: ugh! I hear you talk, and I say to myself: "That man doesn't know how to talk to a lady."

SMIRNOV: You'd like me to come simpering to you in French, I suppose. "*Enchanté, madame! Merci beaucoup* for not paying zee money, *madame! Pardonnez-moi* if I 'ave disturbed you, *madame!* How *charmante* you look in mourning, *madame!*"

MRS. POPOV: Now you're being silly, Mr. Smirnov.

SMIRNOV: (*mimicking*) "Now you're being silly, Mr. Smirnov." "You don't know how to talk to a lady, Mr. Smirnov." Look here, Mrs. Popov, I've known more women than you've known pussy cats. I've fought three duels on their account. I've jilted twelve, and been jilted by nine others. Oh, yes, Mrs. Popov, I've played the fool in my time, whispered sweet nothings, bowed and scraped and endeavoured to please. Don't tell me I don't know what it is to love, to pine away with longing, to have the blues, to melt like butter, to be weak as water. I was full of tender emotion. I was carried away with passion. I squandered half my fortune on the sex. I chattered about women's emancipation. But there's an end to everything, dear madam. Burning eyes, dark eyelashes, ripe, red lips, dimpled cheeks, heaving bosoms, soft whisperings, the moon above, the lake below—I don't give a rap for that sort of nonsense any more, Mrs. Popov. I've found out about women. Present company excepted, they're liars. Their behavior is mere play acting; their conversation is sheer gossip. Yes, dear lady, women, young or old, are false, petty, vain, cruel, malicious, unreasonable. As for intelligence, any sparrow could give them points. Appearances, I admit, can be deceptive. In appearance, a woman may be all poetry and romance, goddess and angel, muslin and fluff. To look at her exterior is to be transported to heaven. But I have looked at her interior, Mrs. Popov, and what did I find there—in her very soul? A crocodile. (*He has gripped the back of the chair so firmly that it snaps.*) And, what is more revolting, a crocodile with an illusion, a crocodile that imagines tender sentiments are its own special province, a crocodile that thinks itself queen of the realm of love! Whereas, in sober fact, dear madam, if a woman can love anything except a lapdog you can hang me by the feet on that nail. For a man, love is suffering, love is sacrifice. A woman just swishes her train around and tightens her grip on your nose. Now, you're a woman, aren't you, Mrs. Popov? You must be an expert on some of this. Tell me, quite frankly, did you ever know a woman to be—faithful, for instance? Or even sincere? Only old hags, huh? Though some women are old hags from birth. But as for the others? You're right: a faithful woman is a freak of nature—like a cat with horns.

MRS. POPOV: Who *is* faithful, then? Who *have* you cast for the faithful lover? Not man?

SMIRNOV: Right first time, Mrs. Popov: man.

MRS. POPOV: (*going off into a peal of bitter laughter*) Man! Man is faithful! that's a new one! (*Fiercely.*) What right do you have to say this, Mr. Smirnov? Men faithful? Let me tell you something. Of all the men I have ever known my late husband Popov was the best. I loved him, and there are women who know how to love, Mr. Smirnov. I gave him my youth, my happiness, my life, my fortune. I worshipped the ground he trod on—and what happened? The best of men was unfaithful to me, Mr. Smirnov. Not once in a while. All the time. After he died, I found his desk drawer full of love letters. While he was alive, he was always going away for the week-end. He squandered my money. He made love to other women before my very eyes. But, in spite of all, Mr. Smirnov, *I* was faithful. Unto death. And beyond. I am *still* faithful, Mr. Smirnov! Buried alive in this house, I shall wear mourning till the day I, too, am called to my eternal rest.

SMIRNOV: (*laughing scornfully*) Expect me to believe that? As if I couldn't see through all this hocus-pocus. Buried alive! Till you're called to your eternal rest! Till when? Till some little poet—or some little subaltern with his first moustache—comes riding by and asks: "Can that be the house of the mysterious Tamara who for love of her late husband has buried herself alive, vowing to see no man?" Ha!

MRS. POPOV: (*flaring up*) How dare you? How dare you insinuate—?

SMIRNOV: You may have buried yourself alive, Mrs. Popov, but you haven't forgotten to powder your nose.

MRS. POPOV: (*incoherent*) How dare you? How—?

SMIRNOV: Who's raising his voice now? Just because I call a spade a spade. Because I shoot straight from the shoulder. Well, don't shout at me, I'm not your steward.

MRS. POPOV: I'm not shouting, you're shouting! Oh, leave me alone!

SMIRNOV: Pay me the money, and I will.

MRS. POPOV: You'll get no money out of me!

SMIRNOV: Oh, so that's it!

MRS. POPOV: Not a ruble, not a kopeck. Get out! Leave me alone!

SMIRNOV: Not being your husband, I must ask you not to make scenes with me. (*He sits.*) I don't like scenes.

MRS. POPOV: (*choking with rage*) You're sitting down?

SMIRNOV: Correct, I'm sitting down.

MRS. POPOV: I asked you to leave!

SMIRNOV: Then give me the money. (*Aside.*) Oh, what a rage I'm in, what a rage!

MRS. POPOV: The impudence of the man! I won't talk to you a moment longer. Get out. (*Pause.*) Are you going?

SMIRNOV: No.

MRS. POPOV: No?!

SMIRNOV: No.

MRS. POPOV: On your head be it. Luka!

(*Enter LUKA.*)

Show the gentleman out, Luka.

LUKA: (*approaching*) I'm afraid, sir, I'll have to ask you, um, to leave, sir, now, um—

SMIRNOV: (*jumping up*) Shut your mouth, you old idiot! Who do you think you're talking to? I'll make mincemeat of you.

LUKA: (*clutching his heart*) Mercy on us! Holy saints above! (*He falls into an armchair.*) I'm taken sick! I can't breathe!!

MRS. POPOV: Then where's Dasha? Dasha! Dasha! Come here at once! (*She rings.*)

LUKA: They gone picking berries, ma'am, I'm alone here—Water, water, I'm taken sick!

MRS. POPOV: (*to SMIRNOV*) Get out, you!

SMIRNOV: Can't you even be polite with me, Mrs. Popov?

MRS. POPOV: (*clenching her fists and stamping her feet*) With you? You're a wild animal, you were never housebroken!

SMIRNOV: What? What did you say?

MRS. POPOV: I said you were a wild animal, you were never housebroken.

SMIRNOV: (*advancing upon her*) And what right do you have to talk to me like that?

MRS. POPOV: Like what?

SMIRNOV: You have insulted me, madam.

MRS. POPOV: What of it? Do you think I'm scared of you?

SMIRNOV: So you think you can get away with it because you're a woman. A creature of poetry and romance, huh? Well, it doesn't go down with me. I hereby challenge you to a duel.

LUKA: Mercy on us! Holy saints alive! Water!

SMIRNOV: I propose we shoot it out.

MRS. POPOV: Trying to scare me again? Just because you have big fists and a voice like a bull? You're a brute.

SMIRNOV: No one insults Grigory S. Smirnov with impunity! And I don't care if you *are* a female.

MRS. POPOV: (*trying to outshout him*) Brute, brute, brute!

SMIRNOV: The sexes are equal, are they? Fine: then it's just prejudice to expect men alone to pay for insults. I hereby challenge—

MRS. POPOV: (*screaming*) All right! You want to shoot it out? All right! Let's shoot it out!

SMIRNOV: And let it be here and now!

MRS. POPOV: Here and now! All right! I'll have Popov's pistols here in one minute! (*Walks away, then turns.*) Putting one of Popov's bullets through your silly head will be a pleasure! Au revoir. (*Exit.*)

SMIRNOV: I'll bring her down like a duck, a sitting duck. I'm not one of your little poets, I'm no little subaltern with his first moustache. No, sir, there's no weaker sex where I'm concerned!

LUKA: Sir! Master! (*He goes down on his knees.*) Take pity on a poor old man, and do me a favour: go away. It was bad enough before, you nearly scared me to death. But a duel—!

SMIRNOV: (*ignoring him*) A duel! That's equality of the sexes for you! That's women's emancipation! Just as a matter of principle I'll bring her down like a duck. But what a woman! "Putting one of Popov's bullets through your silly head . . ." Her cheeks were flushed, her eyes were gleaming! And by God, she's accepted the challenge! I never knew a woman like this before!

LUKA: Sir! Master! Please go away! I'll always pray for you!

SMIRNOV: (*again ignoring him*) What a woman! Phew!! *She's* no sour puss, *she's* no cry baby. She's fire and brimstone. She's a human cannon ball. What a shame I have to kill her!

LUKA: (*weeping*) Please, kind sir, please, go away!

SMIRNOV: (*as before*) I like her, isn't that funny? With those dimples and all? I like her. I'm even prepared to consider letting her off that debt. And where's my rage? It's gone. I never knew a woman like this before.

(*Enter MRS. POPOV with pistols.*)

MRS. POPOV: (*boldly*) Pistols, Mr. Smirnov! (*Matter of fact.*) But before we start, you'd better show me how it's done, I'm not too familiar with these things. In fact I never gave a pistol a second look.

LUKA: Lord, have mercy on us, I must go hunt up the gardener and the coachman. Why has this catastrophe fallen upon us, O Lord? (*Exit.*)

SMIRNOV: (*examining the pistols*) Well, it's like this. There are several makes: one is the Mortimer, with capsules, especially constructed for duelling. What you have here are Smith and Wesson triple-action revolvers, with extractor, first-rate job, worth ninety rubles at the very least. You hold it this way. (*Aside.*) My God, what eyes she has! They're setting me on fire.

MRS. POPOV: This way?

SMIRNOV: Yes, that's right. You cock the trigger, take aim like this, head up, arm out like this. Then you just press with this finger here, and it's all over. The main thing is, keep cool, take slow aim, and don't let your arm jump.

MRS. POPOV: I see. And if it's inconvenient to do the job here, we can go out in the garden.

SMIRNOV: Very good. Of course, I should warn you: I'll be firing in the air.

MRS. POPOV: What? This is the end. Why?

SMIRNOV: Oh, well—because—for private reasons.

MRS. POPOV: Scared, huh? (*She laughs heartily.*) Now don't you try to get out of it, Mr. Smirnov. My blood is up. I won't be happy till I've drilled a hole through that skull of yours. Follow me. What's the matter? Scared?

SMIRNOV: That's right. I'm scared.

MRS. POPOV: Oh, come on, what's the matter with you?

SMIRNOV: Well, um, Mrs. Popov, I, um, I like you.

MRS. POPOV: (*laughing bitterly*) Good God! He likes me, does he? The gall of the man. (*Showing him the door.*) You may leave, Mr. Smirnov.

SMIRNOV: (*quietly puts the gun down, takes his hat, and walks to the door. Then he stops and the pair look at each other without a word. Then, approaching gingerly*) Listen, Mrs. Popov. Are you still mad at me? I'm in the devil of a temper myself, of course. But then, you see—what I mean is—it's this way—the fact is—(*Roaring.*) Well, is it my fault, damn it, if I like you? (*Clutches the back of a chair. It breaks.*) Christ, what fragile furniture you have here. I like you. Know what I mean? I could fall in love with you.

MRS. POPOV: I hate you. Get out!

SMIRNOV: What a woman! I never saw anything like it. Oh, I'm lost, I'm done for, I'm a mouse in a trap.

MRS. POPOV: Leave this house, or I shoot!

SMIRNOV: Shoot away! What bliss to die of a shot fired by that little velvet hand! To die gazing into those enchanting eyes. I'm out of my mind. I know: you must decide at once. Think for one second, then decide. Because if I leave now, I'll never be back. Decide! I'm a pretty decent chap. Landed gentleman, I should say. Ten thousand a year. Good stable. Throw a kopeck up in the air, and I'll put a bullet through it. Will you marry me?

MRS. POPOV: (*indignant, brandishing the gun*) We'll shoot it out! Get going! Take your pistol!

SMIRNOV: I'm out of my mind. I don't understand anything any more. (*Shouting.*) You there! That vodka!

MRS. POPOV: No excuses! No delays! We'll shoot it out!

SMIRNOV: I'm out of my mind. I'm falling in love. I *have* fallen in love. (*He takes her hand vigorously; she squeals.*) I love you. (*He goes down on his knees.*) I love you as I've never loved before. I jilted twelve, and was jilted by nine others. But I didn't love a one of them as I love you. I'm full of tender emotion. I'm melting like butter. I'm weak as water. I'm on my knees like a fool, and I offer you my hand. It's a shame, it's a disgrace. I haven't been in love in five years. I took a vow against it. And now, all of a sudden, to be swept off my feet, it's a scandal. I offer you my hand, dear lady. Will you or won't you? You won't? Then don't! (*He rises and walks toward the door.*)

MRS. POPOV: I didn't say anything.

SMIRNOV: (*stopping*) What?

MRS. POPOV: Oh, nothing, you can go. Well, no, just a minute. No, you can go. Go! I detest you! But, just a moment. Oh, if you knew how furious I feel! (*Throws the gun on the table.*) My fingers have gone to sleep holding that horrid thing. (*She is tearing her handkerchief to shreds.*) And what are you standing around for? Get out of here!

SMIRNOV: Goodbye.

MRS. POPOV: Go, go, go! (*Shouting.*) Where are you going? Wait a minute! No, no, it's all right, just go. I'm fighting mad. Don't come near me, don't come near me!

SMIRNOV: (*who is coming near her*) I'm pretty disgusted with myself—falling in love like a kid, going down on my knees like some moongazing whippersnapper, the very thought gives me gooseflesh. (*Rudely.*) I love you. But it doesn't make sense. Tomorrow, I have to pay that interest, and we've already started mowing. (*He puts his arm about her waist.*) I shall never forgive myself for this.

MRS. POPOV: Take your hands off me, I hate you! Let's shoot it out!

(*A long kiss. Enter LUKA with an axe, the GARDENER with a rake, the COACHMAN with a pitchfork, HIRED MEN with sticks.*)

LUKA: (*seeing the kiss*) Mercy on us! Holy saints above!

MRS. POPOV: (*dropping her eyes*) Luka, tell them in the stable that Toby is *not* to have any oats today.

In reading a play, we must begin to direct it: to imagine the characters and to create the tones in which the lines are said.

As the curtain rises we see a drawing room of a country house that gives the impression someone well-to-do lives here. Mrs. Popov, "small, with dimpled cheeks," is dressed in mourning clothes and stands sighing over a photograph. Luka, "an old man," obviously a servant, hovers nearby. He refers to Mrs. Popov as "ma'am" and talks quite differently from her (". . . like it was a convent. . . ." "My old lady died. . . . I couldn't . . . wail all my life, she just wasn't worth it"). The two characters are from different stations in life, but they are alike in having lost their mates. They are contrasted in the attitudes that they take toward their losses.

The first three speeches serve as exposition. Mrs. Popov has been "moping" for a year in memory of, we assume, the subject of the photograph ("*He* is in his grave."), and she thinks of herself as in a grave, too. Luka thinks that she ought to stop mourning and meet the local regimental officers, while she is still young and pretty

Since Mrs. Popov is young and pretty, her determination to stay in her self-made grave is suspect. We can guess that the author is introducing the element of suspense—will she or won't she? We suspect the latter and remember Luka's comment about meeting the officers. Repeated ideas are like threads holding a play together.

In Mrs. Popov's second speech, we detect a great sense of exaggeration and overstatement. Her speech is so flowery that we begin to suspect the writer does not intend us to take it seriously. We are reminded of the play within a play in *Hamlet*. When Ophelia says that the prologue is brief, Hamlet responds, "As woman's love." When the player queen says to her dying husband that she will never remarry, Hamlet asks his mother how she enjoys the play. Her answer is, "The lady doth protest too much, methinks." Chekhov's lines are a comic replay of such thoughts.

We also find in the second speech that Popov has been unfaithful to his wife. Each subsequent reference to him makes him seem worse and worse. It soon becomes apparent that Mrs. Popov was not loved by her husband. Now that he is gone, she is trying to convince herself that she was loved. Her method is to mourn for Popov more than he was worth.

Since she has now set up an idealized and romantic version

of her love, at variance with reality, she believes that a symbol of that love is the horse Toby. In her mood of foolish sentimentalism, she orders "them to give Toby an extra portion of oats today."

Given this background, we move into a new phase of the play with the ringing of the doorbell and Mrs. Popov's announcement that she is not at home to visitors.

As Luka goes to the door, Mrs. Popov soliloquizes over the photograph of the "naughty boy," and while she is alone, we learn more about his shabby treatment of her. By this time it is quite clear to anyone that Mrs. Popov's lines could be read only in a mock-tragic tone.

But now the "perfect monster" is at the door. Chekhov uses a common device here of having a character talked about before he or she enters, thus raising the expectations of the audience. Mrs. Popov is ready to give him "his come uppance," but first declares, "I *must* enter a convent!" a line that is likely to become ironic as the play develops. The quiet mood changes as Smirnov comes in shouting "Dolt! Idiot!" and then ("*With dignity*") introduces himself. The fact that he is a retired lieutenant reminds us of Luka's earlier statement that Mrs. Popov should meet some soldiers, and the reference to the debt reminds us of Popov's character.

The motif of the oats comes up again, reminding us of Toby and, of course, Mr. Popov. The introduction of the motif at this time alerts us to watch whether Smirnov will be a parallel or a contrast to Popov. That Mrs. Popov asks Smirnov his name three times indicates that she is not paying much attention to him. The actress would probably be moving around, perhaps straightening furnishings, with no more than a glance at her visitor.

The contrast in tones used by Smirnov and Mrs. Popov is suggested partly by the author's stage directions ("*shouting*") ("*sweetly*"), and can also be inferred from what the two characters say—"What the hell do I care about your steward?" and "What a tone to take to a lady!" Then Mrs. Popov walks out, insulted.

For a while Smirnov shouts after her; then ("*Quietly, as he realizes he's talking to air*") goes into a soliloquy, orders vodka, and continues his soliloquy. He talks of "the logic of women!

... Creatures of poetry and romance!" His voice rises and falls. He shouts out the window that his horse is to have oats (with a contrasting intention to Mrs. Popov's ordering oats for Toby), tells us what he himself looks like, and is ready to "grind the whole world to powder." Here, again, we can suspect that this last thought may become ironic before the curtain falls.

In the midst of his soliloquy, Smirnov says, "You won't get around *me* with your widow's weeds [clothes for mourning] and your schoolgirl dimples." He indicates here that he has looked more carefully at her than she has at him. Luka, in an aside, says, "There's an evil spirit abroad. The Devil must have sent him. Oh!"

Mrs. Popov reenters with a silly speech about her "rural retreat," and a request that Smirnov not "break the silence." But why is she "looking at the floor"? Is her attitude changing?

Smirnov decides to stay until he is paid and then remembers that he needs the money now. Mrs. Popov continues to demand the respect due to a "lady."

Smirnov then makes his long speech on woman, recapitulating his search for romance and finding that a woman has the soul of "a crocodile that thinks itself queen of the realm of love." The two argue over whether a man or woman is most likely to be faithful. Mrs. Popov points out the failures of her late husband, her own faithfulness, and her withdrawal from life. But Smirnov ("*laughing scornfully*") makes fun of her; her faithfulness will last until "some little poet—or some little subaltern with his first moustache—comes riding by."

That remark sets Mrs. Popov "*flaring up*." Since people get most angry when told what they suspect to be the truth, we can assume that perhaps Mrs. Popov is not sure of her own position. Is her withdrawal a pose?

The romantic speeches are over, and the pace picks up with the short lines and each character shouting at the other. In the meantime poor Luka is blubbering in the background, adding to the general confusion. Smirnov, after being told that he is not "housebroken," proves it by challenging Mrs. Popov to a duel.

Mrs. Popov's reaction is magnificent; we see her suddenly in a new light, ready to put a bullet through Smirnov's "silly head." While she gets the guns, the tone of the lines changes in Smirnov's speech on "women's emancipation," ending in "I never knew a woman like this before." During that soliloquy the actor must change from an angry tone to one of new admiration for this woman.

Then we get a scene that is an actor's delight. When Mrs. Popov asks for directions on how to shoot a pistol, really asking how to kill Smirnov, he must somehow get behind her and begin giving directions as he holds her arm—as well as show that he is falling in love. Then he announces to the audience, "My God, what eyes she has! They're setting me on fire." And to her he says, "I'll be firing in the air." When she asks him to leave, what changes her mind?

How will the actor deliver the two speeches beginning, "Shoot away!" and "I'm out of my mind"? How will Mrs. Popov say, "Take your hands off me, I hate you! Let's shoot it out!"?

As Luka, the gardener, the coachman, and the hired men come to the rescue, the scene ends with the line, "Toby is *not* to have any oats today," reminding us of the other references to oats and suggesting the questions, What does the reference mean this time? What threads of the play does it pull together?

EXERCISE

At first glance, Mrs. Popov and Smirnov are unlike: one seemingly ready for the convent, the other a "brute." As the play develops, we can see that they are much alike. On this last point, we can make some notes on their similarities:

1. They are in low moments in their lives: Mrs. Popov thinks that she is ready for the convent; Smirnov must pay his own debt and suggests that he will hang himself if he cannot.
2. They are brought together by their relationships with Popov.
3. Both have had unhappy love affairs.
4. Each is short-tempered.
5. Both are pretending to be something that they are not: he, a woman-hater; she, a faithful lover.
6. They are very blunt in their ways of speaking.
7. Each is in an absurd position: one ready to stay forever; the other mourning a no-good husband.
8. Both are romantics.

Using these notes, modifying them as you like, write a paper on the play. You may use the two opening sentences of this exercise as an introduction to your paper. Make clear what you take the notes to mean; clarify the terms when necessary. Prove what you say about the two characters with specific references to the play.

APPENDIX

APPENDIX

HOW TO INTRODUCE QUOTATIONS INTO YOUR PAPERS

In your papers you should quote sparingly and skillfully. You can avoid overquoting by paraphrasing an author's words and indicating the source of your ideas. If you do quote, keep the number of words as brief as possible. Here are some ideas that may be helpful.

Short quotations (fifty words or less) can be run into your own text, but they must be enclosed in quotation marks.

> When Donovan talks of duty, Bonaparte says, "I never noticed that people who talk a lot about duty find it much of a trouble to them." Hawkins argues that he never "let down a pal."

Avoid quotations that merely repeat in the author's words what you have already said.

> The burial took place in the dark "with nothing but a patch of lantern-light between ourselves and the dark."

If you need to explain something that is not clear in the context of the paper, use brackets [ ], not parentheses ( ), for your comments.

> Her husband said, "But she's so astonishingly pretty."
> Her husband said, "But she's [the visiting girl] so astonishingly pretty.

(In the first example, it may not be clear to a reader who "she" is. In the second example, the writer adds his own explanation in brackets.)

The effect of the killing is shown in the comment, "I [Bonaparte] was somehow very small and very lost and lonely like a child astray in the snow."

If your quotation is more than fifty words, separate the quotation from the body of the paper by skipping three lines of type; then indent four or five spaces. Single-space your quoted material without using quotation marks, unless the quotation itself contains quotation marks.

At one point in the story, Maupassant comments on the peasant's predicament:

> He went home, ashamed and indignant, choked with rage, with confusion, the more cast-down since from his Norman cunning, he was, perhaps, capable of having done what they accused him of, and even of boasting of it as a good trick. His innocence dimly seemed to him impossible to prove, his craftiness being so well known.

Short quotations are usually introduced by a comma; longer ones by a colon (see above example) or sometimes by a period.

When confronted by Donovan's talk of duty, Belcher says, "I never could make out what duty was myself."

An example can be seen in the first four lines of John Keats's "To Sleep";

> O soft embalmer of the still midnight,
> Shutting, with careful fingers and benign,
> Our gloom-pleased eyes, embowered from the light,
> Enshaded in forgetfulness divine;

Quotations of less than fifty words are sometimes set off as above if they are of special importance and need to be emphasized.

Follow exactly the wording, spelling, and punctuation of anything that you quote. You can, however, vary the capitalization to a limited extent.

The hostages were told that "there were four of our fellows shot. . . ."

(The original sentence being quoted read, "There were four of our fellows. . . ."

> Bonaparte said, "It was worse on Noble than on me."

(The original read, "I had the feeling that it was worse on Noble than on me.")

Or you can begin with an ellipsis (. . .), indicating that part of the quotation is missing.

> Bonaparte said, ". . . it was worse on Noble than on me."

When an ellipsis is used to indicate the omission of words, it may come at the beginning, within, or at the end of a quotation. Note that if the ellipsis comes at the end, it is followed by the punctuation that is at the end of the quoted sentence.

> "Noble says he saw everything ten times the size, as though there were nothing in the whole world by that little patch of bog . . . , and I was somehow very small and very lost and lonely like a child astray in the snow."

> "Then, by God, in the very doorway, she fell on her knees and began praying. . . ."

You must use an ellipsis if you leave out something in the middle of a quotation. At the beginning and end of a quotation you may omit the ellipsis. Whichever method you choose, be consistent.

When a quotation ends, the period or comma goes inside the quotation mark. The question mark is put inside if it is a part of the quotation.

> She asked her husband, "Philip, am I pretty?"

QUOTING LINES OF POETRY

If two or three lines of poetry are quoted in your text, separate each with a slanting line (/).

Blake refers to "the invisible worm / That flies in the night / In the howling storm."

More than two lines of poetry may be indented and quoted in the same way as prose lines.

Blake addresses himself to the rose, saying,

> O Rose, thou art sick.
> The invisible worm
> That flies in the night
> In the howling storm.

(The period after "storm" does not appear in the original. Here it marks the end of the sentence in the essay.)

Any quotation, including the words that introduce it, must make a grammatically complete and correct sentence.

Wrong: Donovan says that he is "only doing our duty." (The pronouns do not agree.)
Right: Donovan says that "we're only doing our duty."
Wrong: Bonaparte "opened my eyes at the bang."
Right: Bonaparte said, "I opened my eyes at the bang."

A 3
B 4
C 5
D 6
E 7
F 8
G 9
H 0
I 1
J